Why Greatness Cannot

Kenneth O. Stanley • Joel Lehman

Why Greatness Cannot Be Planned

The Myth of the Objective

 Springer

Kenneth O. Stanley
Department of EECS
   Computer Science Division
University of Central Florida
Orlando, FL, USA

Joel Lehman
Department of Computer Sciences
The University of Texas at Austin
Austin, TX, USA

The image on the cover has been used with permission from the University of Central Florida
Research Foundation, Inc. It was created using the www.picbreeder.org website of UCFRF.

ISBN 978-3-319-15523-4   ISBN 978-3-319-15524-1   (eBook)
DOI 10.1007/978-3-319-15524-1

Library of Congress Control Number: 2015932228

Springer Cham Heidelberg New York Dordrecht London

Springer International Publishing AG Switzerland is part of Springer Science+Business Media (www.
springer.com)

To Beth and Bennett
KS

To my parents
JL

Preface

This book was born from a radical idea about artificial intelligence (AI) that unexpectedly grew to be about much more. At first I was thinking only about AI algorithms, programs of concern mainly to computer scientists like me. Usually these algorithms have explicit goals and objectives that they're driven to achieve. But I began to realize that the algorithms could do amazing things even if they had no explicit objective—maybe even more amazing than the ones that did have an objective. Testing this idea led to some surprising experimental results, some of which are documented in this book. And that's pretty interesting—if you're a computer scientist.

But then something unusual happened. I started to realize that the insight wasn't just about algorithms, but also about life. And not just life, but culture, society, how we drive innovation, how we plan for achievement, our interpretation of biology— the list just kept expanding. If you don't understand why I say that's unusual, just consider how rare or bizarre it is for a computer algorithm to change how you think about life. After all, you don't fall into an existential crisis every time you boot up your laptop. The unexpectedly broad implications of the idea surprised me, so at first I kept them tucked quietly in the back of my head—but they kept getting louder.

As a professor, I'm sometimes invited to give public talks on my research. So as an experiment, when I spoke publicly about the idea I began touching on its relationship to our lives and society. And as I saw how people reacted and how much passion it provoked, the message took on a new life—because I could see it had meaning well beyond the field of its origin. So I realized someone had to write this book at least to try to communicate the novel insight. And that's why you're in for a unique experience in the pages ahead. There is a story here—a story about an idea in AI and how it grew into something bigger—but there's also a journey through a dizzying set of surprisingly broad implications for everything from personal dating, to the march of science, to the evolution of the human brain. I hope you'll enjoy this whirlwind tour across a landscape of once familiar concepts—but now observed through a psychedelic new lens.

One more important detail about the history of this project—it was really a two-person effort. From the earliest experiments to realizing the growing set of implications, my coauthor Joel Lehman was instrumental all along the way. The ideas here are the result of years of exchange and debate between the two of us, and the book is therefore truly a joint effort. So from the first chapter onward, we'll be speaking with a single unified voice as we guide you through *Why Greatness Cannot Be Planned: The Myth of the Objective.*

Joel and I would both like to express gratitude to the institutions that supported this work: the University of Central Florida, the University of Texas at Austin, and the Santa Fe Institute, where I completed the book while on sabbatical. Every past and current member of the Evolutionary Complexity Research Group at UCF deserves special thanks for their input and ideas over the years. I am also indebted to Gary Leavens, the Chair of the Computer Science Division at UCF, who encouraged me to make this book a reality. This book also probably would not have happened without the motivation provided by early invitations to speak from Richard Gabriel of IBM Research (at the 2010 SPLASH conference) and Seung Chan Lim (Slim) of the Rhode Island School of Design in 2011. For creating the experiment that provided the initial inspiration for the ideas in this book, the entire Picbreeder team and later Picbreeder contributors deserve special mention: Jimmy Secretan (lead), Nick Beato, Adam Campbell, David D'Ambrosio, Adelein Rodriguez, and Jeremiah T. Folsom-Kovarik; Nazar Khan, Peter Matthews, and Jan Prokaj later contributed to researching Picbreeder's color extension.

*   *   *

The book is organized into two parts for the convenience of different readers. The first part of the book (the first nine chapters) constructs the main argument against objectives and provides general evidence for their cost in a number of areas of life and society. For readers interested in more elaborate implications of the myth of the objective in specific scientific fields (in particular biology and artificial intelligence), two additional case studies are included at the end of the book. That way, while you can absorb the main ideas from just the first nine chapters, these additional case studies provide further depth for those who desire more.

Santa Fe Institute, Santa Fe, NM   Kenneth Stanley
March 10, 2015

Contents

Chapter 1
Questioning Objectives

*Now, in his heart, Ahab had some glimpse of this, namely: all
my means are sane, my motive and my object mad.*

Herman Melville, *Moby Dick*

Imagine waking up without thinking about what you need to do today. Have you ever done that? Suppose then you go to work, but instead of holding the usual meetings and poring over benchmarks and milestones, your boss instead tells you to *do whatever you feel is most interesting*. What would you do? When you later check the news online, there is no talk of national testing standards or missed objectives for the economy. Strangely enough, teachers somehow still teach and money somehow still changes hands anyway. Maybe you post a profile on a dating website, but you leave blank all the answers on what you look for in a partner. Today you aren't looking for anything in particular, but that still doesn't stop you from looking. While you probably won't experience a day like this one anytime soon—a day without objectives—what would life be like if you could? Would it be confusing, difficult to navigate, too open-ended—or, quite the opposite, a lot *better*?

It's interesting that we rarely talk about the dominance of objectives in our culture even though they impact us from the very beginning of life. It starts when we're barely more than a toddler. That momentous first day that we enter kindergarten is the gateway to an endless cycle of assessment that will track us deep into adulthood. And all that assessment has a purpose—to measure our progress towards specific *objectives* set for us by society or by ourselves, such as mastering a subject and obtaining a job. The reality is that objectives lurk in the background from the earliest moments. But they only start there. Over the years they keep gathering steam, eventually enveloping practically everything we do.

If you want evidence for that, all you need to do is stop in at your local bookstore and take a look at the magazine rack. There you will be reminded that you might want to *change jobs, lose 15 pounds, start a company, find a date, get promoted, change your look, make a million dollars, buy a house, sell a house,* or even *complete a video game*. In fact, almost anything worth doing is expressed as an objective. Now, we're not suggesting by any means that all of these objectives are a waste of time. Of course, many are admirable. Others may be more frivolous, but whatever you may think of one objective or another, we rarely question the value of

© Springer International Publishing Switzerland 2015
K.O. Stanley, J. Lehman, *Why Greatness Cannot Be Planned*,
DOI 10.1007/978-3-319-15524-1_1

framing all our pursuits with objectives. Can you imagine life with fewer objectives, or with no objectives at all? Would it lead to any good? Regardless of how you'd answer these questions, at the least they highlight how deeply our culture has come to revere objectives.

And it's not only about individual pursuits. While it's true that children are graded for their progress towards mastering a subject, the schools themselves are *also* graded. But in the case of the schools, their objective is to produce high student test scores. Even nations set objectives, like low crime, low unemployment, and low carbon emissions. A lot of effort and resources are spent measuring progress towards these objectives and others like them. There's an assumption behind these pursuits that isn't often stated but that few would think to question: We assume that any worthy social accomplishment is best achieved by *first* setting it as an objective and *then* pursuing it together with conviction. It makes you wonder, is there such a thing as accomplishment without objectives?

If you take a look at most professions, the answer would appear to be no. Take engineers for example. They typically set objectives through rigorous specifications. Then they continually measure how their prototypes compare to these specifications. Inventors are similar, conceiving an invention and then pursuing it as an objective. In the same spirit, scientists must come up with clear objectives to secure funding for their projects, which are then judged by how likely they are to achieve their objective. The list goes on. Investors set earnings objectives and corporations set profit objectives. Even artists and designers often mentally conceive a design and set its realization as their objective.

The weight of objectives on our thinking even impacts the way we talk about topics like animals in nature. After all, whenever evolution is discussed, we view animals through the lens of *survival and reproduction*, evolution's assumed objective. Even many *algorithms*, or programs that run inside computers, are designed to work towards some specific objective, such as finding the best search result or playing a better game of chess. In fact, these kinds of algorithms are quite common in artificial intelligence and machine learning. So it may come as no surprise that the term *objective function* is now practically a household name in such fields.

Maybe all this objective mania makes sense. At some level, we must believe it does to have allowed it to dominate our lives so completely. Or maybe it's something else—maybe we've become so used to objectives defining everything we do that we've forgotten that their value can even be questioned. Either way, there's a certain appeal to this kind of routine. The idea that all our pursuits can be distilled into neatly-defined objectives and then almost mechanically pursued offers a kind of comfort against the harsh unpredictability of life. There's something reassuring about the clockwork dependability of a world driven by tidy milestones laid out reliably from the starting line.

Though often unspoken, a common assumption is that the very act of setting an objective creates possibility. The very fact that *you put your mind to it* is what makes it possible. And once you create the possibility, it's only a matter of dedication and perseverance before you succeed. This can-do philosophy reflects how deeply optimistic we are about objectives in our culture. All of us are taught that hard work and dedication pay off—if you have a clear objective.

Even so, perhaps you've felt qualms about this kind of thinking from time to time. It might sound good on the face of it, but what it *leads to* isn't always so comforting—legions of measurements, assessments, metrics—woven into every aspect of our lives. It's like we've become slaves to our objectives, toiling away towards impossible perfection. Objectives might sometimes provide meaning or direction, but they also limit our freedom and become straitjackets around our desire to *explore*. After all, when everything we do is measured against its contribution to achieving one objective or another, it robs us of the chance for playful discovery. So objectives do come with a cost. Considering that this cost is rarely discussed in any detail, maybe it's a good idea to look a little harder at what we're really giving up in exchange for such objective optimism.

But before we do, it's important that you know that we aren't pessimists. It may sound like this book is going in a cynical direction, but that isn't really true. In fact, we believe that human achievement has no limits. It's just that we're going to highlight a different path to achievement, without the need for objectives. There's a lot our culture has sacrificed in the name of objectives, and we're going to take it back. They've stolen our freedom to explore creatively and blocked us from serendipitous discovery. They ignore the value of following a path for its own uniqueness, rather than for where it may lead. The chapters ahead will show that great discoveries are lurking just beyond our fingertips, if only we can *let go* of the security blanket of the objective. Sometimes, the best way to change the world is to stop *trying* to change it—perhaps you've noticed that your best ideas are often those you were not seeking. We'll come back to this paradox later, but first let's think a little more about the way most people approach achievement today.

*   *   *

It usually starts with deciding on an objective. In a lot of professions, the first question you'll hear if you propose a new project is, "What is the objective?" People often say that a particular pursuit is not "well-defined" enough unless you can tie it to an objective. That's usually the only way to prove your idea is worth considering. For example, even if you have a strong hunch that combining two chemicals will lead to an interesting reaction, hardly any scientist will take you seriously unless you can *define* what that interesting reaction would be. Only then could you say that you have a clear objective, and a legitimate pursuit is underway.

Sometimes a word other than "objective" might be used, but usually it plays a similar role. For example, scientists often demand *hypotheses* from each other because they don't want to fund research only because it sounds "interesting." "What is the hypothesis?" they'll insist. It's similar to asking what is the objective. Without a hypothesis, an experiment is reduced to *mere speculation*, little more than child's play. The hypothesis, like the objective of any project you might want to pursue, certifies that it's worth pursuing. Even if it might not work out, it still provides a clear outcome that will allow people to judge your success or failure later.

This attitude doesn't only apply to business or science. It's personal too. If you join a dating site, you're supposed to know what you want and what you like, so that you can describe what you're "looking for." If you're starting college, you're supposed to figure out your major so that you have a clear body of knowledge to pursue. And as any high school student realizes who is applying to college, even hobbies are supposed to have *some* kind of purpose. "Staring at the wall" will not meet much respect on a college application, even if it's when you have your best ideas.

Whether you're an executive, a scientist, a student, or even just a single looking for a date, once your objective is defined usually the next step is to put all your energy into achieving it. In other words, we pull out all the stops in the pursuit of our goal. But there's actually one other ingredient in pursuing an objective that is not as obvious but almost always present: Usually progress towards the objective is somehow *measured*. This is where all the measurements and metrics of our culture come into play. The purpose of all the measuring is to help us figure out whether we're heading in the right direction. If things aren't going well, it gives us the chance then to switch directions. For example, in school the objective is to master a subject. Grades are a measure that tell us whether we're making progress in that direction. So if your grades in school are going down, you may need to change your approach to studying.

There's a useful word that comes from optimization theory that some scientists use to describe this idea of using a measure to help decide what to do next—they call the measure a *gradient*. It's basically a clue to which direction is right and which is wrong. We all quickly become very familiar with following such gradients, to the point that it almost becomes unconscious by the time we're adults. The "hot and cold" children's game is a perfect introduction to the idea: The young contender searches for a hidden treasure known only to the other players, who provide clues by saying "hotter" or "colder." The idea is so simple that children naturally follow the "gradient" of increasing temperature with little need for explanation (and definitely no need to learn anything about optimization theory). As long as the gradient is going up, chances are that success is coming closer. In a sense we never stop playing the hot and cold game. The process of setting an objective, attempting to achieve it, and measuring progress along the way has become the primary route to achievement in our culture.

Obviously we're going to raise a lot of questions about the benefits of objectives, but one important point is that we're mainly focused on *ambitious* objectives—those whose achievement is anything but certain. One of the reasons that objectives aren't often questioned is that they work perfectly well for more modest pursuits. If a manufacturer decided to increase efficiency by 5 %, no one would be shocked if it succeeded. A software company upgrading its product from version 2.0 to version 3.0 is similarly likely to succeed, as happens all the time. Everyday successes like these mislead us into believing that setting objectives works well for almost *everything*. But as objectives become more ambitious, reaching them becomes less promising—and that's where the argument becomes most interesting.

Some objectives are anything but certain. Medical researchers have yet to cure cancer. And it's hardly clear that computer scientists will succeed in creating a convincingly-human artificial intelligence any time soon. It would be nice to have a limitless source of energy with no risk or environmental impact whatsoever, but who knows when that will happen. Even fully immersive holographic television, which you must admit would be fun though perhaps less noble, is nowhere in sight. Maybe there is even a beautiful new genre of music waiting to be found, so enchanting that all of humanity would succumb to its spell, if only the right artist can find it. Or, if you want to get *really* ambitious, how about time travel or teleportation? You might even have some big ones of your own, like making a billion dollars. Of course some ambitious objectives might turn out impossible. But *some* are possible, and if we could even come close to achieving them, the world would surely change for the better.

The question then is, *how will we ever get there?* How can we achieve not just improving our golf swing, but our *dreams*? These are the kinds of questions where objectives offer less assurance. After all, even if time travel is theoretically possible, the best use of national resources at this moment is surely not to reroute trillions of dollars into an all-out effort to build a time machine. But why not? Is setting the objective not the first step towards success? Or would pursuing time travel be our Moby Dick, distracting us from what really matters in life?

*   *   *

Why is it so hard to achieve ambitious objectives? To get a handle on the problem, think about all the things that are *possible*. As an example, consider all possible *images*. Everything you've ever seen falls into this class, but so do many things you've never seen and will never see. Now consider this: A minuscule proportion of all possible images are great masterpieces like Leonardo da Vinci's *Mona Lisa* or Vincent Van Gogh's *The Starry Night*. These are objectives that are hard to achieve. A larger proportion of possible images are recognizable but less inspiring than the masterpieces, like pictures of acquaintances and everyday objects. Of course, the vast majority of possible images are of no interest whatsoever—like television screens tuned to the wrong channel, just random static. One exciting aspect of this vast set of all possible images is that some of the great masterpieces *do not yet exist* because no one has painted or drawn them yet. Put another way, these future masterpieces are not yet *discovered*.

It's useful to think of achievement as a process of discovery. We can think of painting a masterpiece as essentially discovering it within the set of all possible images. It's as if we are *searching* through all the possibilities for the one we want, which we call our objective. Of course, we're not talking about search in the same casual sense in which you might search for a missing sock in the laundry machine. This type of search is more elevated, the kind an artist performs when exploring her creative whims. But the point is that the familiar concept of search can actually make sense of more lofty pursuits like art, science, or technology. All of these pursuits can be viewed as searches for something of value. It could be new art, theories, or inventions. Or, at a more personal level, it might be the search for the right career.

Whatever you're searching for, in the end it's not so different from any other human process of discovery. Out of many possibilities, we want to find the one that's right for us.

So we can think of creativity as a kind of search. But the analogy doesn't have to stop there. If we're searching for our objective, then we must be searching *through* something. We can call that something the search *space*—the set of all possible things. Now try to picture this space—it's as if different possibilities appear at different locations in a big room. Imagine this giant room in which every image conceivable is hovering in the air in one location or another, trillions upon trillions of images shimmering in the darkness, spanning wall to wall and floor to ceiling. This cavernous room is the space of all possible images. Now imagine walking through this space. The images within it would have a certain *organization*. Near one corner are all kinds of faces, and near another are starry nights (and somewhere among them Van Gogh's masterpiece). But because most images are just television noise, most of the room is filled with endless variations of meaningless gibberish. The good stuff is relatively few and far between.

The nice thing about thinking of discovery in terms of this big room is that we can think of the process of creation as a process of searching through the space of the room. As you can imagine, the kind of image you are most likely to paint depends on what parts of the room you've already visited. If you've never seen watercolor, you would be unlikely to suddenly invent it yourself. In a sense, civilization has been exploring this room since the dawn of time. As we explore more and more of it, together we become more aware of what is possible to create. And the more you've explored the room yourself, the more you understand where you might be able to go next. In this way, artists are searching the great room of all possible images for something special or something beautiful when they create art. The more they explore the room, the more possibilities open up.

Let's pretend you wanted to paint a beautiful landscape—so that's your objective. If you're experienced in landscape painting, it means that you've visited the part of the room teeming with images of landscapes. From that location, you can branch off to new areas full of landscapes that are still unimagined. But if you're unfamiliar with landscape painting, unfortunately, you're unlikely to create a masterpiece landscape even if that's your objective. In a sense, the places we've visited, whether in our lives or just in our minds, are *stepping stones* to new ideas.

This way of thinking doesn't only work for paintings. We can imagine a room filled with anything. For example, it could be a giant room full of inventions. As with images, the great room of all possible inventions is mostly filled with inelegant doodads, like unreliable machines that occasionally can move a ball from one location to another and pointlessly ring a bell. But if you look hard enough, some areas of the room contain simple yet useful ideas—bags, wheels, wheelbarrows, spears. Rarer still are more sophisticated inventions—in one corner are all manner of cars and in another corner, computers. Somewhere in the room are fanciful machines unlike any we've seen before, still waiting to be found.

Let's visit the pocket of space filled with computers. If you spend a lot of time in this area, an interesting thing begins to happen: You start to understand the shape of the space, how one computer leads to another, like stepping stones along a winding path. Wander here long enough, and you might even start to see where the interesting possibilities may lie.

But why do we have to wander? Why can't we just go directly to the location of the most powerful machine of all? The reason is that the only clue to the future is found in the past. The first computer, the ENIAC, was introduced in 1946 and could execute 5,000 instructions per second [1]. While this might sound like a lot, a modern desktop computer executes over *ten billion* instructions per second [2]. In other words, ENIAC was a slug, more than two million times slower than today's computers.

You might wonder, why didn't the designers simply set their objective to build a fast computer in 1946? After all, we now know it's possible. Why start so slow? But the world always works this way. Before anyone had explored the part of the great room filled with computers, no one could know what was even possible there. You have to visit before you can depart. In short, the stepping stones to faster computers were not yet known in 1946 because they had not yet been *discovered*, just as we do not yet know the stepping stones that may lead to computers two million times faster than today's. Stepping stones are portals to the next level of possibility. Before we get there, we have to find the stepping stones.

The moral of course is that objectives have to be realistic for us to have the hope of reaching them. The idea of a large imaginary "room" whose space is being searched is a metaphor that helps to see why this principle holds. It's no surprise then that computer scientists even have a term, *search space*, that refers to this very concept—it's the general idea that creation and discovery happen within a space of possibilities that contains stepping stones leading from one discovery to another. The big question when setting ambitious objectives is always whether we can find a path through this search space from where we currently are to where we want to be in the future—the path to the objective.

Sometimes, figuring out the path from here to the objective isn't exactly a major challenge. For example, if your objective is to eat, you probably won't need to explore very much to figure out that you need to visit the refrigerator before making a sandwich. But the paths to many objectives are of course a lot more difficult to guess. If you're a freshman in college, there may be a path to making a million dollars before you reach 30, but what you should do first is probably not so obvious. In other words, you'll have to *search* for the right stepping stones, and if you're lucky and clever enough, you might discover the ones that lead to the objective. There may be a number of stepping stones you have cross, and many of them are likely challenging to figure out.

*   *   *

Now we can finally tell you what this book is really about. It's not just about achievement or how to succeed. The deeper message here is about a surprising paradox. We'll have a lot more to say on it in later chapters, but you can get the gist of it just from what we've said so far: Objectives are well and good when they are sufficiently modest, but things get a lot more complicated when they're more ambitious. In fact, objectives actually become *obstacles* towards more exciting achievements, like those involving discovery, creativity, invention, or innovation—or even achieving true happiness. In other words (and here is the paradox), the greatest achievements become *less likely* when they are made objectives. Not only that, but this paradox leads to a very strange conclusion—if the paradox is really true then the best way to achieve greatness, the truest path to "blue sky" discovery or to fulfill boundless ambition, is to have *no objective at all*.

Why would this be? The key problem is that the stepping stones that lead to ambitious objectives tend to be pretty strange. That is, they probably aren't what you would predict if you were thinking only of your objective. Put another way, if you were walking through one of these great rooms of all possible things, how the items in the room are arranged would be unpredictable and confusing. History is full of examples of this vexing problem. For example, the very first computer was built with vacuum tubes, which are devices that channel electric current through a vacuum. However, here's the strange part: The history of vacuum tubes has nothing to do with computers. People like Thomas Edison who were originally interested in vacuum tubes were investigating electricity, not computing. Later, in 1904, physicist John Ambrose Fleming refined the technology to detect radio waves, still with no inkling of building a computer. It was only decades later that scientists first realized that vacuum tubes could help build computers, when the ENIAC was finally invented [3].

So even though vacuum tubes are a key stepping stone on the road to computers, few if any could see it coming. In fact, if you were alive in 1750 with the objective of building some kind of computer, you'd never think of inventing a vacuum tube first. Even *after* vacuum tubes were first discovered, no one would realize their application to computation for over 100 years. The problem is that *the stepping stone does not resemble the final product.* Vacuum tubes on their own just don't make people think about computers. But strangely enough, as history would have it vacuum tubes are right next to computers in the great room of all possible inventions—once you've got vacuum tubes you're very close to having computers, if only you could see the connection. The problem is, who would think of that in advance? The arrangement, or *structure*, of this search space is completely unpredictable.

Unfortunately, this kind of unpredictability is the rule rather than the exception in almost any situation with an ambitious objective. The first engine was not invented with airplanes in mind, but of course the Wright brothers needed an engine to build a flying machine. Microwave technology was not first invented for ovens, but rather was part of magnetron power tubes that drove radars. Only when Percy Spencer first noticed the magnetron melt a chocolate bar in his pocket in 1946 did it become clear that microwaves are stepping stones to ovens [4].

These stories of delayed revelations and serendipitous discovery expose the danger of objectives: If your objective was to invent a microwave oven, you would not be working on radars. If you wanted to build a flying machine (as countless failed inventors did over the years), you wouldn't spend the next few decades instead trying to invent an engine. If you were like Charles Babbage in the 1820s [5] and wanted to build a computer, you wouldn't dedicate the rest of your life to refining vacuum tube technology. But in all these cases, what you would never do is exactly what you should have done. The paradox is that the key stepping stones were perfected only by people *without* the ultimate objective of building microwaves, airplanes, or computers. The structure of the search space—the great room of all possible things—is just plain weird. It's so bad that the objective can actually *distract* you from its own stepping stones! If you think too much about computers you'll never think of vacuum tubes. The problem is that ambitious objectives are often *deceptive*. They dangle a false promise of achievement if we pursue them purposefully. But strangely in the end we often must give them up ever to have the chance of reaching them.

This paradox isn't just about historical events. It applies just as much today as ever—to everything from society's greatest challenges to your own personal ambitions. Chances are that if we plan a path based on our objective, then it will miss the stepping stones. This insight raises some troubling questions that relate to the tricky nature of stepping stones: Do increasing test scores really lead to subject mastery? Is the key to artificial intelligence really related to intelligence? Does taking a job with a higher salary really bring you closer to being a millionaire? Is cancer going to be cured by an insight from someone who is not a cancer researcher? Are improvements in television technology bringing us any closer to holographic television?

It often turns out that the *measure* of success—which tells us whether we are moving in the right direction—is deceptive because it's blind to the true stepping stones that must be crossed. So it makes sense to question many of our efforts on this basis. But actually the implications are even more grave than just questioning particular pursuits and their objectives. At a deeper level, we might ask why we think ambitious pursuits should be driven by objectives *at all*.

*   *   *

It's not hard to find great ideas that were never objectives for anyone, at least not until almost the moment they were discovered. Rock and roll music took inspiration from jazz, blues, gospel, and country music. In a way, those genres acted as stepping stones to rock and roll. But no one was *trying* to discover rock and roll because no one knew it even existed as a possibility. Jazz musicians weren't trying to influence the birth of rock any more than ragtime composers consciously tried to shape jazz. Even so, strangely enough, ragtime *did* shape jazz and jazz did shape rock and roll.

Count Basie, who was a respected name in jazz during the birth of rock and roll, described how new musical styles really come about: "If you're going to come up with a new direction or a really new way to do something, you'll do it by just playing your stuff and letting it ride. The real innovators did their innovating by just being themselves." The funny thing is that not only was it completely unpredictable in the early twentieth century that jazz and blues would lead to rock and roll, but no one was even worried about it because *rock and roll was not an objective*. We just happened to be traveling the right path through the search space of musical genres to bump into it in the late 1940s [6].

One of the biggest names in popularizing rock and roll is of course Elvis Presley. Interestingly, his unmistakable sound wasn't planned either. Guitarist Scotty Moore recalls, "All of a sudden, Elvis just started singing this song, jumping around and acting the fool, and then Bill picked up his bass, and he started acting the fool, too, and I started playing with them. ... [the recording engineer] stuck his head out and said, 'What are you doing?' And we said, 'We don't know [6].' " Who would have thought that "acting the fool," and not some ambitious drive to overhaul popular music, would transform the world of rock and roll? The stories of Elvis and rock and roll in general illustrate that not only can objectives block discovery, but that *having no objective* can lead to the greatest discoveries of all.

However, the problem is that it's hard to simply abandon objectives because they are a powerful security blanket. At the least they *seem* to protect us from the wild unknowns of the world. They give us a sense of purpose and the promise of success if only we try hard enough. No doubt, the thought of aimlessly wandering through the space of possibilities with no clear purpose is not going to inspire many can-do achievers. But that is not where this argument leads. We don't face a false choice between slavishly following objectives and aimless wandering. Instead, the true implications are both more subtle and more liberating than that. We want to show you that it's possible to explore a search space intelligently even without an objective. In other words, there *is* a third way—just because you don't have an objective doesn't mean you have to be wandering. We can align ourselves towards discovery and away from the trap of preconceived results.

Over the remainder of this book an important principle will begin to emerge: Sometimes the best way to achieve something great is to stop trying to achieve a *particular* great thing. In other words, greatness is possible if you are willing to stop demanding what that greatness should be. While it seems like discussing objectives leads to one paradox after another, this idea really should make sense. Aren't the greatest moments and epiphanies in life so often unexpected and unplanned? Serendipity can play an outsize role in life. There's a reason for this pattern. Even though serendipity is often portrayed as a happy *accident*, maybe it's not always so accidental after all. In fact, as we'll show, there's a lot we can do to attract serendipity, aside from simply betting on random luck.

We hope you'll find this message liberating. Our world has become saturated with objectives and metrics for success that mechanize our lives and distract us from our passions. But there are other paths to happiness and success. We'll show you why not only can you trust your gut instinct when it tells you something important is around the corner, but you *should* trust it, even if you can't explain what that something is. You don't need to make up a tortured *reason* to justify every little impulse you feel. And not only is this attitude more healthy for us as humans anyway, but it's backed up by solid scientific evidence that this book will present. We're missing out on a lot by clinging to objectives.

The objective culture around us is not natural anyway. How many children do you know who formulate an objective before they go out to play? How many great scientists really formulated a hypothesis *before* their great idea? Do you ever tell yourself that you can't do something because it's not *justified* by a clear purpose?

Do you ever blame yourself when you can't achieve your highest goals despite your best efforts? Why do so many of us feel our creativity is stifled by the machine-like integration of modern society? We weren't born for this. It isn't healthy for us, and deep down we know that. Something is wrong at a fundamental level with the assumptions that justify where our time is invested.

At the same time, this book is not only about personal liberation. In fact, objectives have become so pervasive that their absence would impact nearly everything. Their absence can change how science is conducted, how engineers conceive their projects, how architects generate new concepts, and how designers seek success. It can alter our understanding of natural evolution and how computer scientists develop algorithms. It can turn engineering into art and art into science. It can build bridges between disciplines and break down walls between others. It can redefine entrepreneurship and refocus our targets for investment. It can teach humility to the overconfident and confidence to the insecure. In short, objectives are a pillar of our culture, but they're also a prison around our potential. It's time to break out and discover what's outside.

Both of us, Ken and Joel, are computer scientists by training. Neither of us originally set out to attack or even question a topic so universal and seemingly solid as the benefits of objectives. Instead, we were (and still are) interested in artificial intelligence (AI), which was our primary area of expertise. However, it's funny how you never know where your path might lead, just like the theme of this book. It turns out that even in the field of AI objectives are everywhere. Many of the computer programs that AI researchers develop are designed to follow one objective or another, almost as if they're mimicking our own culture's drive to define success in the same way. For example, the objective for an AI program might be to help a robot learn to travel through a maze. With the field of AI itself so immersed in objectives, perhaps it was inevitable at some point that researchers in AI would eventually have to confront the downside of objectives themselves.

For us, the realization that there is a deep and largely unrecognized problem with objectives came from a particular AI project that we'll talk about in the third chapter. But the problem is a lot bigger than just about AI. It's about how you choose your major, find your spouse, and choose your profession. It's about how we make great discoveries, and how we pass our free time. It relates to happiness and success, but it's not even just about those things. It's also about understanding what really leads to major advances and major successes. Because once we understand that, our perspective can really change, and maybe then we can all spend more time on what's important and less time worrying about the myth—*the myth of the objective.*

Chapter 2
Victory for the Aimless

Life is what happens to you while you're busy making other plans.

John Lennon

Sometimes things work out the way we intended. Sometimes you study accounting and become an accountant. Or maybe you play basketball as a kid and make it onto the varsity team. But the great successes, the ones that come crashing out of nowhere and shake up the system, they don't usually follow this kind of script. You don't enroll in Superstar 101 to become a superstar. There's no magic formula for changing the world. In other words, the greatest victories are not written into the initial plans. They happen despite the plans.

Take career choice for example. There's no shortage of resources to help you choose your target career. You can read Richard Bolles' *What Color Is Your Parachute?* to find out how to choose and secure the job that's right for you [7]. Or you could take the *Career Key* test to discover what you really should be doing with your life [8]. The list is endless. There's the *Campbell Interest and Skill Survey* [9], personality tests like the *Myers-Briggs Type Indicator* [10] and *Keirsey Temperament Sorter* [11], skillset assessments, work values tests, and so on. Amazon.com shows over 97,000 books on careers. If you can't find your way, there's always a guru eager to guide you.

But while a little guidance may be good for some, others don't follow the script. Some people set objectives and completely miss them—all for the better. Why is this kind of story so common for the most successful? Why don't they need to stop in at a career counselor? At heart, it's not such a mystery. It's just that anticipating what might lead to the most fulfilling outcomes is difficult. As with all open-ended problems in life, the stepping stones are unknown. So when you go out into the uncertain world sometimes it may be wise to hitch a ride with serendipity. Being open and flexible to opportunity is sometimes more important than knowing what you're trying to do. After all, any path might lead to happiness, even the most unexpected. Some people seem to have an uncanny knack for spotting such opportunities, even if they conflict outright with their original aims.

© Springer International Publishing Switzerland 2015
K.O. Stanley, J. Lehman, *Why Greatness Cannot Be Planned*,
DOI 10.1007/978-3-319-15524-1_2

In an interesting experiment by Richard Wiseman [12], subjects were asked to count the number of photographs in a newspaper. It turns out that those who focused on the goal of counting the photographs took significantly *longer* to complete the task than those who were less focused on the objective. Why? The more open-minded participants noticed that on the inside of page two Wiseman had written, "Stop counting: There are 43 photographs in this newspaper." While some might say that noticing the answer on page two is only luck, the deeper lesson is that focusing too much on your goal can actually prevent you from making useful unexpected discoveries.

Some might also say Johnny Depp was just lucky. Who would have guessed that being in a mildly successful band would somehow lead to an incredibly successful career in acting? Wouldn't it be smarter to fill your schedule with hours of acting classes? But starting a band was the right stepping stone for Johnny Depp, though not so much because it was logical or planned. It was simply that Depp wanted to make music and was open to opportunities when they came. In fact, even his high school principal once told him to pursue his dream of musical stardom instead of finishing high school. While his music career never blossomed, it turns out that joining a band had some unexpected benefits. Not only did Depp marry the bass player's sister, but she ultimately introduced him to acting through her job as a makeup artist [13]. If Johnny Depp had not wanted to become a musician, he may never have become an actor.

For the very successful, these kinds of stories are surprisingly common. Before he wrote books, the bestselling novelist John Grisham first trained and practiced as a criminal defense attorney for ten years. The trigger for his career change was particular testimony that he overheard one day from a young rape victim. Somehow that testimony made him realize that he should and could write, and he began waking early in the morning before work to gradually complete his first novel, *A Time to Kill* [14]. His next book, *The Firm*, would spend 47 weeks on the New York Times bestseller list. Most aspiring writers would not choose law school to develop their craft. Reading endless case studies in a dusty library seems like poor preparation compared to practicing creative writing. But maybe that's why it worked for John Grisham. He wasn't following a plan.

In fact, that seems to be a pretty good strategy if you want to be a writer. Before *Harry Potter* sold millions of copies, J.K. Rowling was a bilingual secretary for Amnesty International and then taught English to students learning it as a second language in Portugal [15]. Haruki Murakami, the Japanese writer behind such award-winning reveries as *The Wind-Up Bird Chronicle* and *Kafka on the Shore*, first ran a combination coffee house and jazz bar. Murakami himself is convinced that without running the bar he never would have become a writer because it gave him the time to observe and brood. Many of his characters later shared his fondness for jazz. Interestingly, it didn't occur to Murakami that he could write novels until he was 29 [16].

And the examples keep coming. The founder of American hard-boiled detective fiction, Raymond Chandler, didn't write until he was fired from his job as an oil company executive at age 45 [17]. And as late-blooming philosopher Mary Midgley said, "I wrote no books until I was a good 50, and I'm jolly glad because I didn't know what I thought before then [18]." So if you want to be a top writer, perhaps you shouldn't try to be a writer.

Of course there are always the guardians of objective thinking who want to thwart our deeper desires. They'll tell us to be practical and set more realistic objectives. For some reason, musicians seem to confront this problem a lot. John Lennon's mother provided this bit of wisdom: "The guitar's all very well, John, but you'll never make a living out of it [19]." Elton John faced similar advice from his father, who wanted to talk him out of his "implausible wish to become a 'star' [20]." The pressure to choose *realistic* objectives is familiar to all of us. Just think of the common saying, "Get your head out of the clouds." While the pressure to be practical clearly affects musicians, their stories reflect a wider cultural assumption: Following a path for its raw attraction is sillier than following it for its practicality.

In some cases, the seed of greatness is planted long before it blossoms. Harland David "Colonel" Sanders cooked for his family as a six-year old after his father's death, but would not make a living out of it until he was 40. In between, he tried his luck at piloting a steamboat, selling insurance, and even farming. But the opportunity for success didn't arrive until he owned a gas station, where he began cooking chicken for his customers [21]. No one could have predicted that such a winding road of careers would eventually lead to Kentucky Fried Chicken, but one thing is clear: Harland Sanders had no problem catching the winds of serendipity— he exhibited a willingness to switch his direction throughout his early life—and it paid off.

The common thread in all these tales is that the successful wander from their original paths, whether those paths were chosen by themselves or others. Somehow, what seemed originally the right objective became merely a stepping stone to a different horizon. Whether it's Johnny Depp's love of music unexpectedly pulling him into acting or John Grisham's legal experience inspiring him to write, we never know how far away the stepping stones might lead. Somehow successful people are *open* to falling off the path. Instead of blind devotion to their original objective, their secret ingredient seems to be a willingness to make a complete 180 when the feeling is right. And as we can see, the results can be spectacular.

You might think these kinds of stories only apply to the luckiest of the lucky. But serendipity isn't actually so picky. A peer-reviewed study found that nearly two thirds of adults attribute some aspect of their career choice to serendipity [22]. As one participant put it, "I happened to visit an animal hospital and became interested in veterinary medicine." You never know what hidden passion you might unexpectedly discover.

Some career experts are beginning to take this trend seriously. As one large survey revealed, "actions such as volunteering, joining clubs and generally making contact with other people and groups are likely to increase a client's chances of an unplanned experience [23]." Note the emphasis on *unplanned* experience. This isn't the usual attempt to figure out the best job and pursue it as an objective. It isn't an impersonal test designed to categorize you into a particular box from a few multiple choice questions. Instead it suggests that you should embark on a search for possible stepping stones without any particular destination.

*   *   *

The beauty of this non-objective principle is that it's not only about careers. It can apply to almost anything that involves searching for something, which covers an enormous range of activities. Because the stepping stones that lead to the greatest outcomes are unknown, not *trying* to find something can often lead to the most exciting discoveries (or self-discoveries). This same theme of finding without trying to find will emerge repeatedly throughout this book everywhere from computer simulations to educational systems.

Who would have thought that so many disparate scenarios would follow this strange yet fundamental principle? The key is to be open to change, to a shifting landscape where appearances can be deceiving yet liberating at the same time. The great achievers are willing to abandon their original objectives and spring for opportunity when it arises. What is important in these scenarios is to avoid locking into rigid commitment to the original ambitious objective, and instead remaining mindful and open to where the present stepping stone might lead. Sometimes all it takes is sensing potential—whether it be in becoming a musician or finding a new way to cook—even if the true nature of that potential is still unknown.

While the idea that not looking can be the best way to find is strange and perhaps a bit zen, it does lurk already in some corners of our culture. As Loretta Young said, "Love isn't something you find. Love is something that finds you." As one of those great elusive objectives that almost all of us seek, it's easy to relate to the deceptive search for love. But the funny thing is that almost any ambitious objective could be substituted for the word "love" in the wisest statements uttered on the topic. We just seem to have carved out this small niche, the search for love, where we acknowledge the paradox of ambitious objectives. As D.H. Lawrence put it, "Those that go searching for love, only manifest their own lovelessness. And the loveless never find love, only the loving find love. And they never have to seek for it [24]."

Many people sooner or later realize that preconceived notions about the ideal partner often end up surprisingly unsatisfying [25]. But what is this realization really about in the bigger picture? The deeper issue, which affects all kinds of objectives beyond just love, is that the true nature of the greatest discoveries is often far different from how we imagined. That's why the stepping stones are so deceptive—we're comparing them to the wrong ideal.

With love we are all too familiar with this kind of problem. Perhaps that's why love stories are so often surprising and entertaining. They demonstrate that the best results don't need to come from trying to achieve anything, which is fun because such light-hearted whimsy so sharply contrasts with how we're taught to pursue our dreams. For example, one day Grace Goodhue was watering flowers only to look up and see Calvin Coolidge in the window shaving with nothing on but underwear and a hat. Luckily for him, she laughed, catching his attention [26]. It's unlikely that the future Ms. Coolidge ever targeted men who shave in their underwear, or that future President Coolidge ever thought his best moment would involve being caught almost naked. But then again, the unplanned is often the best plan of all. At least in the domain of romance, we all have some experience with the paradox of ambitious objectives. After all, what could be more ambitious than seeking lifelong happiness?

Just as that lesson is familiar for love, it's also sometimes present in other spheres, like our recreations. For example, unlike with careers we often choose hobbies not because of some long-term grandiose plan, but just because we like them. So again having no objective leads at least to some personal satisfaction. The Internet has made it easier now to share and discover odd hobbies like "snail racing," "underwater hockey," "limbo skating," "extreme unicycling," and even "extreme ironing" (all of which you can find on Wikipedia). Some hobbies do even become stepping stones to something bigger—Nathan Sawaya was a corporate attorney who had so much fun building artistic models out of Lego blocks that he quit his job to do it full time [27]. But despite the risks of deviating from his original plan, following his heart in this case led again to something better and now his unique pieces sell well enough to make a good living.

Or maybe you've heard of Joseph Herscher, who spends much of his time building intricate Rube Goldberg machines with no real necessity other than being fun to watch [28]. In one contraption, a ball rolls down a ramp and falls onto a lever that lights a fuse, burning away a string that releases another ball and so on, all ultimately accomplishing nothing but opening his newspaper. It might sound pointless (a popular word for having no clear objective) but as usual there are considerable benefits: His work has been viewed by millions, leading to numerous television and radio appearances. Indeed, psychologists have noted that children need time to explore without specific tasks or objectives set for them by adults [29, 30]. Sometimes the term *unstructured play* is used to describe this kind of activity. Maybe adults need it too.

Of course, when you hear about people spending their adult lives playing with Legos or building Rube Goldberg machines, it's easy to dismiss their passions as frivolous. But there's a deeper value to such endeavors than just the endeavors themselves: They reflect that we don't know which stepping stones might lead to something interesting. These are people who are willing to commit their lives to stepping stones that most of us would entirely ignore, which is good for all of us. Because no one knows the stepping stones that lead to the greatest discoveries, the last thing we want to do is stop people from exploring stepping stones that we ourselves choose to ignore—who knows what they will find? It's not that we are all one day going to wake up desperately seeking Rube Goldberg machines. But what if Joseph Herscher one day wakes and realizes that one of his Rube Goldberg machines solves an unexpected problem?

A historical example of just this kind is given by the unexpected discovery of ancient cave paintings by a non-scientist, Marcelino de Sautuola, near the hill of Altamira in Spain in 1879 [31]. Before this discovery, people had no idea of how sophisticated prehistoric paintings could be. Importantly, Marcelino held a wide variety of unique hobbies, including caving and learning about ancient artifacts.

By lucky coincidence these hobbies coincided when he explored a cave discovered by a hunter, and his daughter noticed paintings of bison on the ceiling of the cave. He realized their significance and alerted a professor friend. Without the hobbies that he pursued mainly for fun, those paintings might never have been found. Unexpectedly, these hobbies became stepping stones to great discoveries.

When his daughter first peered at those paintings, Marcelino realized suddenly that fun wasn't the only benefit of his recreational activities. Interestingly, this kind of pivot is fairly common behind the scenes of many success stories, such as in today's Internet businesses. Oftentimes a website created for one purpose only turned a profit after being taken in a new direction outside of the original plans. For example, YouTube was first envisioned as a video dating site [32]. But when was the last time you found a date through YouTube? Its founders pivoted to video sharing, and the results speak for themselves. And speaking of sharing, the photo sharing service Flickr was originally a smaller feature of a bigger social online game (that itself was inspired by playing an unrelated game about virtual pets) [33]. It turned out that the photo-sharing feature outshined the social game it was part of. Of course, pivoting companies aren't unique to the Internet age. For example, the (now) video-game company Nintendo also took a winding path to its success. Founded in 1889, for years Nintendo made a modest profit selling traditional Japanese playing cards. Later in the 1960s, as the playing card market collapsed, the company nearly went bankrupt trying out new business ventures like running a taxi service, building short-stay "love hotels," manufacturing instant rice, and selling toys. The manager of the new toys and games division, Hiroshi Imanishi, hired a group of amateur weekend tinkerers to brainstorm products. When one of the tinkerers created an extendable mechanical toy hand, Hiroshi was impressed and released it as the "Ultra Hand." The product's huge commercial success prompted the company to abandon its non-toy ventures. Later Nintendo began to explore electronic toys, eventually leading it to become the iconic video game company behind "Super Mario Brothers [34]."

If you take one thing from this chapter, perhaps it should be that you have the right to follow your passions. Even if they deviate from your original plans or conflict with your initial objective, the courage to change course is sometimes rewarded handsomely. Another important implication is that not everything in life requires an objective justification. If you had a choice either to attend a prestigious law school or to join an art colony and chose the latter, your family and friends might have some questions: "Why did you give up such a lucrative career for something so uncertain? What are you trying to accomplish?" Instead of struggling to formulate some kind of objective justification that explains how you have the whole thing completely planned out, perhaps the best answer is that no one knows the stepping stones that lead to happiness. Yes, law school may reliably lead to *money*, but happiness (perhaps for you) is a more ambitious end, and something about that colony feels closer to it. Of course life is full of risk and some choices indeed won't work out, but few achieve their dreams by ignoring that feeling of serendipity when it comes. You can simply tell your friends that you know a good stepping stone when you see one, even if (like everyone) you don't know where it leads.

Whether you're looking for a career, for love, or trying to start companies, there is ample evidence that sticking to objectives just isn't part of the story in many of the biggest successes. Instead, in those successes there is a willingness to serve serendipity and to follow passions or whims to their logical conclusions. But is there any proof beyond just a set of inspiring anecdotes? In fact, it turns out that we stumbled upon this principle originally through a scientific experiment, as the next chapter reveals, involving hundreds of users on the internet breeding pictures.

Chapter 3
The Art of Breeding Art

I will not follow where the path may lead, but I will go where there is no path, and I will leave a trail.

Muriel Strode, from the poem Wind-Wafted Wild Flowers, 1903

This book is about questioning the value of objectives. But how do you begin to question something as basic and common as having an objective? Before the recent ideas that led to writing this book, it's not as if your authors had spent our lives in the thriving anti-objective protest movement (there is no such movement, thriving or otherwise). We just went about our business setting objectives and following them as happily as everyone else. In the meantime, we were researchers in artificial intelligence, looking for ways to make smarter machines. How we went from there to writing a book against objectives is a strange story that helps to explain the origin of the equally strange idea that objectives might often cause more harm than good.

The story of this book really began when our research group decided to build a website called Picbreeder that was also a unique kind of scientific experiment. At first, the idea behind Picbreeder had little clear connection to objectives. In fact, it was originally conceived as a place where visitors could literally breed pictures. While that may not make sense when you first hear it, it's actually a simple idea. The plan was to make it work roughly like animal breeding: Pictures on the site would be able to have "children" that are slightly different from their parents (just as animals have children that are unique but still clearly related to their parents). The hope was that by allowing visitors to breed the pictures they find most interesting, over time they would end up breeding works of art that please them, even if the visitors themselves were not artists.

Of course, at first glance, a website for breeding art sounds bizarre. How can art be bred? A Picasso painting can hardly seduce a Van Gogh. But actually there is a way it can make sense. The key to understanding Picbreeder is that when real animals are bred together, their *genes* are combined to form their offspring. It turns out that scientists in artificial intelligence have found a way to create an artificial "DNA" for pictures stored inside computers. The result is that you can breed the genes of these pictures together just like those of animals. This technology, first introduced by Richard Dawkins in his book *The Blind Watchmaker* [35], is sometimes called *genetic art*. Since Dawkins' original demonstration of the idea

© Springer International Publishing Switzerland 2015
K.O. Stanley, J. Lehman, *Why Greatness Cannot Be Planned*,
DOI 10.1007/978-3-319-15524-1_3

scientists have significantly enhanced its capabilities, which is part of what inspired us to make a website where people all around the world can play with it.

To understand genetic art it helps to think of animal breeding. Imagine that you have a stable of horses. If you're the breeder, then you can decide which stallions and mares will mate, and eleven months later there will be a new generation of fresh-maned newborns. The important thing is how you choose the parents. For example, if you wanted fast horses, your strategy might be to choose two fast parents to mate. Of course, you don't have to choose parents only for practical reasons. Maybe you just want the prettiest horses to mate, or the silliest. Whatever the reason, by choosing the parents you influence the children's genes. They naturally end up a mix of the parents' genes. In the next generation, when all the children you bred grow up, the process can be repeated. And some of the children might end up even faster or sillier than their parents. Over many generations, the animals evolve in a way that reflects the choices of their breeder.

Genetic art programs work in much the same way as breeding horses, except that instead of choosing *animals* to breed, you choose *pictures*. What happens is that you see a set of pictures on the screen (perhaps there could be 10 or 20 pictures displayed together at the same time). Then you click on the ones you like, which become the parents of the next generation of pictures. For example, if most of the pictures look circular but you click on the one picture that looks more square, then the next generation will likely contain many square-like images (Fig. 3.1). In other words, square parents make square babies, just as your children might have eyes that look like yours. But like in nature, the offspring don't look *exactly* like their parents. There are slight mutations hidden in their genes, though of course you can still see the resemblance.

If you continue to play this kind of game over and over again, clicking on images you like so that they reproduce to form new images, over many generations the

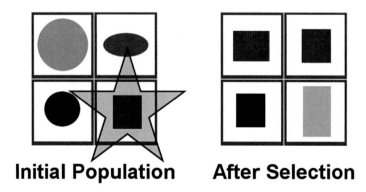

Fig. 3.1 The user selects a square. In this simple example of picture-breeding, the user selects the square-like image in the initial population. As a result, the next generation (at *right*, after selection) contains variations on the square theme because each image is a descendant of the chosen square.

images will evolve in a way the reflects your choices, just as with the horses. Playing with genetic art can be fun because it allows you to explore a lot of possibilities you might never have imagined on your own.

So what does any of this have to do with objectives? There actually is a connection, though it took some time for us to really appreciate it. The objective comes in when you think about where you hope the breeding will lead—that's your objective. For example, with horses your objective might be to breed a fast horse. On Picbreeder, you might want to breed a picture of a face, or an animal. What turned out to be really surprising is that Picbreeder visitors almost always bred the best images when those images were *not* their objective. In other words, Picbreeder seemed to work best when visitors were open minded about what they hoped to find. To see how we can be sure of that, and why it ultimately relates to the impact of objectives in many facets of life, it helps to understand a few details on how the site is set up.

                    *   *   *

In 2006, we had developed a new kind of artificial picture DNA that produced more rich, meaningful images (which you will soon see) than were possible before. But more importantly, this new project, which would become Picbreeder, included another ingredient that made it particularly interesting: Any internet user could *continue* breeding images that were bred by previous users. This feature was critical to Picbreeder because a big obstacle for systems of this type is that their users can only stand to play for a little while at a time before becoming mentally tired [36]. After all, how long could you tolerate staring at a screen full of pictures in one sitting? It turns out that after 20 generations or so (i.e. after choosing parents 20 times in a row), most people simply can't continue concentrating. But evolution works best over many generations, and 20 isn't enough to produce really interesting pictures.

Jimmy Secretan, then a Ph.D. student attending our research group meetings, suggested a clever solution to this problem: Make Picbreeder into an online service. That way, users could *share* images they had previously evolved with other users, who could then continue breeding them. In other words, if you evolved a triangle on Picbreeder, you could publish it to the website, and then someone else could continue breeding it and perhaps discover an airplane. In Picbreeder, this kind of handoff from one user to another is called *branching*. The great thing about branching is that it allows breeding to continue far beyond the 20-generation limit. Tired users can continually hand their current product to a fresh new user to add yet another 20 generations to its lineage. Eventually, these linked chains of handoffs can build up to hundreds of generations of evolution.

But for those who don't want to branch from any previous image, the alternative is to *start breeding from scratch*, which is how every discovery on the site ultimately began. Starting from scratch randomly constructs artificial DNA (from scratch), which ends up producing a bunch of simple random blobs on your screen. From among those blobs, you can pick a parent blob for the next generation of pictures. Figure 3.2 shows what it looks like for a user to start from scratch. You can see that

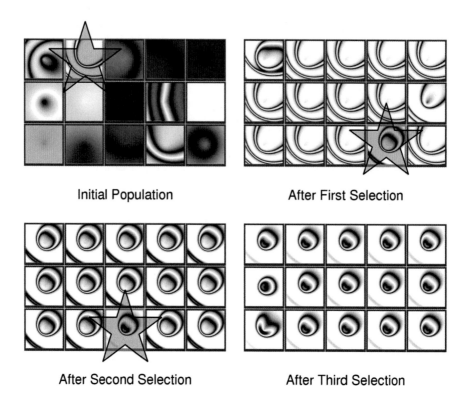

Initial Population   After First Selection

After Second Selection   After Third Selection

Fig. 3.2 A sequence of three selection steps in Picbreeder starting from scratch. As the user selects images, he influences the direction of evolution towards images that please him. The *star* indicates which picture the user selects, which is the parent of the offspring images shown in the next step.

the user evolved a curvy blob into a more circular form with a mouth-like shape inside it. Perhaps interesting, but not an earth-shattering discovery.

But how impressive do you think these pictures could become if you kept breeding them in this way, picking parents generation after generation? It turns out that they become more remarkable than you might expect. Believe it or not, every image in Fig. 3.3 was bred in this way on Picbreeder, all originally going back to random blobs. What's more, the breeders of these images weren't trained artists. They were just curious people who had found the Picbreeder website. In fact, likely few (if any) of them could draw the pictures that they had bred.

Seeing visitors breeding these kinds of images piqued our curiosity. Even with the new artificial DNA, we hadn't realized how lifelike and meaningful the images would become. In a sense, each one of the images in Fig. 3.3 is a unique *discovery*. It's important also to recall that Picbreeder users often continue breeding from each other's discoveries. For example, the skull-like image in the middle of the second row in Fig. 3.3 was evolved in this way. It's actually the result of two users branching off of each other's published images five times in total (for a total of 74 combined

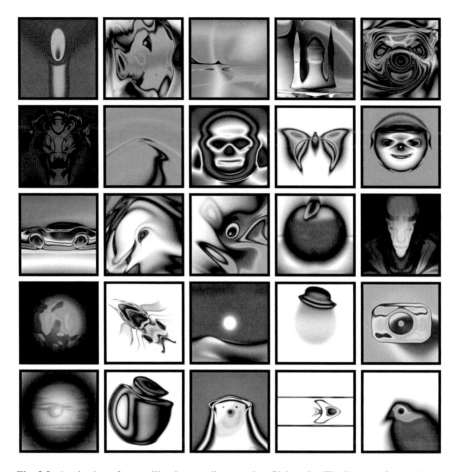

Fig. 3.3 A selection of compelling images discovered on Picbreeder. The lineage of every image in this gallery traces back to a randomly-generated blob.

generations since the initial random-blob ancestor). So even if the final user who evolved an impressive image didn't start from scratch, one of her predecessors must have, which means that in the end everything traces back to random blobs. That gives you a sense of how unlikely these discoveries are.

Now here's where the story gets interesting. Say, for example, that you're in the mood to evolve a picture of the Eiffel Tower. One thing you might think is that if you visit Picbreeder and just keep choosing images to breed that look increasingly like your objective (the Eiffel Tower), eventually you'd find it. But interestingly, it doesn't actually work that way. It turns out that it's a bad idea to set out with the goal of evolving a specific image. In fact, once you find an image on Picbreeder, it's often not even possible to evolve the *same* image again from scratch—even though we *know* it can be discovered!

We confirmed this paradoxical aspect of the system by running a powerful computer program for thousands of generations. First, we chose a target image from those that users have discovered and published on the site. Then, at every generation the program automatically chose parent pictures that look increasingly similar to the target image [37]. The result for the most interesting images—total failure. It's impossible to breed an image if it's set as an objective. The only time these images are being discovered is when they are *not* the objective. The users who find these images are invariably those who were *not looking for them.*

We can give you a specific example because one particularly surprising image— the *Car* on the left side of the third row in Fig. 3.3—was discovered by Ken. So we know the precise story of how it was found. The most important fact: Ken was *not* trying to breed a car. Instead, he had actually chosen to branch from an *Alien Face* image (Fig. 3.4) that had been bred by a previous user. Instead of thinking about cars, Ken originally intended to breed more alien faces. But what happened next— what always happens before a major discovery on Picbreeder—was serendipity: Random mutations caused the eyes of the *Alien Face* to descend gradually over several generations of breeding and suddenly it was apparent that the eyes could be wheels (Fig. 3.5)! Who would have thought that an alien face can lead to a car? But it turned out to be just the right stepping stone.

That story would be merely an interesting anecdote if not for the fact that almost every attractive image on the site follows the same story of serendipity. There is always a surprise stepping stone leading to an unexpected discovery. For example, look at all the bizarre stepping stones in Fig. 3.6. As we began to notice this trend, it was hard to avoid its strange and surprising moral: If you want to find a meaningful image on Picbreeder, you're better off if it is *not* your objective.

In fact, the only reason these discoveries are being made at all is because users are unwittingly laying stepping stones for each other every time they publish a new picture on the site. The user who evolved the *Alien Face* never imagined it might one day lead to a car, and neither did the user (Ken) who eventually evolved the *Car*. No one saw the *Car* coming. So it's a good thing that someone did evolve the *Alien Face*

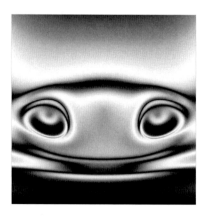

Fig. 3.4 The *Alien Face* image.

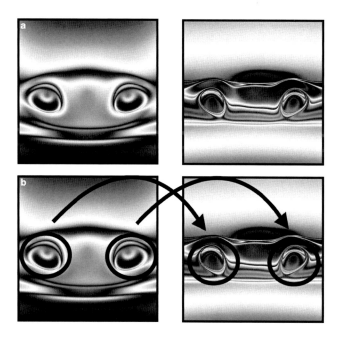

Fig. 3.5 Alien eyes as the precursors of car wheels. The *highlights* and *arrows* illustrate the hidden similarity between the key features.

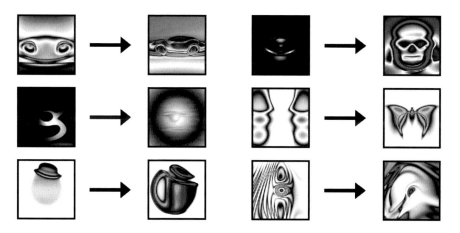

Fig. 3.6 The stepping stones rarely resemble the final products. The images on the *left* are stepping stones along the path to the images on the *right*, despite their dissimilar appearances.

and publish it, because otherwise there would never have been a car (and perhaps no book!). The system works as a whole because it has *no unified objective*—everyone is following their own instincts. And the most successful users of all are those with open minds, who avoid looking for only one thing in particular.

In other words, the most successful users have no objective. When this fact emerged from studying the discoveries made on the site, it was completely unexpected. You would think that the best breeders would be the ones who conceived an objective image (i.e. something they want to evolve) and then bred towards it, but it turns out to be the opposite—the best discoveries on Picbreeder are always the ones that are unplanned. And this initial observation turned out to apply to much more than just pictures.

After all, why should Picbreeder be different than anything else in life? There's something you want to create or to achieve, so you start working on finding the stepping stones that lead you there. But how can you be sure that the stepping stones actually look anything like your ultimate objective? What if they are instead like the *Alien Face*, full of potential, but entirely unlike where they ultimately could lead (like the *Car*)? In that case, if you concentrate too much on achieving your objective, you'll end up ignoring the most critical steps to reaching it. Could it really be, we wondered, that this principle, first observed on an obscure picture-breeding website, actually impacts every aspect of life concerned with achieving objectives? If it does, then it must be important, because objectives are everywhere. And as you saw from all the examples in the last chapter, the same story seems to emerge in many facets of life.

But no matter how many stories we show you with this kind of plot, it still doesn't fully answer *why* the world works this way. That's what the next chapter is about. Yes, abandoning objectives is often the best decision, but there's a reason for this pattern, which is that the stepping stones almost never resemble the final destination, whether planned or not. In other words, no matter how tempting it is to believe in it, the distant objective cannot guide you to itself—it is the ultimate *false compass*.

Chapter 4
The False Compass

> There remains one a priori fallacy or natural prejudice, the most
> deeply-rooted, perhaps, of all which we have enumerated: one
> which not only reigned supreme in the ancient world, but still
> possesses almost undisputed dominion over many of the most
> cultivated minds... This is, that the conditions of a phenomenon
> must, or at least probably will, resemble the phenomenon itself.
>
> John Stewart Mill, *A System of Logic, Ratiocinative and Inductive*

You probably don't often face the problem of crossing a lake on foot by hopping from stepping stone to stepping stone, but imagine if you did. To make life a little harder, suppose also that the lake is covered in mist. The stepping stones closest to the shore fade gradually as they wind into the fog. As you walk along the course of stepping stones over the water, the shore dissolves from sight behind you even as the other side remains cloaked behind the mist. But here's the hard part: Eventually you come upon a fork where a choice must be made.

Because of the fog, you don't know where either path leads. For all you know, one might lead you to a dead end while the other eventually might reach the other side of the lake. But even if you make a lucky choice, chances are that more forks will appear sooner or later. When crossing stepping stones in a fog, many critical decisions must be made with little knowledge of where they lead.

Lakes aren't the only place where this problem comes up. *Stepping stones* arise repeatedly in the discussion of Picbreeder too. In any large, uncharted search space, stepping stones represent the waypoints that must be crossed to eventually reach the objective. In fact, the term "stepping stone" is meant to remind us of this idea of crossing a lake on small stones protruding through the water. The fundamental problem of search and discovery is that we usually don't know the stepping stones that lead to the objective at the outset. After all, if we always knew the stepping stones, then everything we hope to achieve would be easy. Because of such uncertainty, the lake we're crossing is often shrouded in mist. In a sense, the human condition is that we're marooned on a stepping stone with only the insight of the human mind to guide us. Though the mind is a powerful force in search, it's still difficult to see farther than one stepping stone away, no matter our intelligence.

© Springer International Publishing Switzerland 2015
K.O. Stanley, J. Lehman, *Why Greatness Cannot Be Planned*,
DOI 10.1007/978-3-319-15524-1_4

The 30-ton ENIAC computer of 1946 was a key stepping stone on the path to personal computers, but it would take more than 25 years and many intervening models before desktops began to appear [38].

The problem of predicting stepping stones becomes especially hard for ambitious objectives. If you're on the beach making a sandcastle, it's clear that sculpting a stable foundation will support the first sand-caked turret. But the stepping stones between a mud hut and a skyscraper are far less clear, and in fact took centuries for humanity to cross. Another way to look at the challenge of ambitious problems is to say that their solutions are *more than one stepping stone away*. While gifted visionaries often can lead us to the next stepping stone, can anyone guide us all at once beyond the horizon, many stepping stones away?

It turns out that there's a good explanation for why stepping stones are so difficult to predict, which connects to the general problem with objectives. Recall from Chap. 1 that a key tool for pursuing objectives is to *measure* progress towards them. For example, higher marks in school measure progress towards mastering a subject. We expect an "A" student to know more about chemistry than one who is failing the class. To borrow a term from computer science and optimization theory, this kind of measure is often called the *objective function*. Of course it's no surprise that this term includes the word "objective" within it: It's literally a method to measure progress towards the objective. So if we say that the objective function is improving, it means that our measure of progress suggests we're moving closer to the objective. But here's the problem: The idea that an improving score guarantees that you're approaching the objective is wrong. It's perfectly possible that moving closer to the goal actually *does not* increase the value of the objective function, *even if the move brings us closer to the objective.*

This predicament sounds strange. Why would the objective function not register that we're moving in the right direction? But of course the objective function (or any measure of progress) is going to be imperfect because imperfect human beings are the ones who have to come up with the measure. A very common type of objective function does no more than compare our current state directly to the objective. The more it resembles the objective, the higher the score we give it. This common approach reflects the rule of thumb that when you reach a fork in the road it's always better to take the road that heads in the direction of your desired destination. But if you think about the story of the *Car* in Picbreeder, of course this approach would often be misleading. Recall that the predecessor to the *Car* was the *Alien Face*. If our objective function for obtaining a picture like the *Car* is "how car-like is it?" then the *Alien Face* would be graded poorly because alien faces are definitively *not* cars. But the *Alien Face* in fact *was* the stepping stone to the *Car*, which shows you why always comparing *where you are* to *where you want to be* is potentially dangerous.

This situation, when the objective function is a false compass, is called *deception*, which is a fundamental problem in search. Because stepping stones that lead to the objective may not increase the score of the objective function, objectives can be deceptive. It's as if you were hopping across the stepping stones on the foggy lake with a broken compass. If the compass is wrong then it can deceive you, so you might never reach the other side of the lake.

To make this idea more concrete, there's a great example of this kind of deception called the *Chinese finger trap*. The trap is a harmless-looking puzzle shaped as an open tube. To begin, you stick your index fingers into each end. But once inserted, your fingers become trapped—and the harder you try to pull them out, the tighter the trap ensnares them. The deception of the Chinese finger trap is that the path to freedom is to push *inward*, away from freedom. In other words, the stepping stone to freedom is to become *less* free. This situation illustrates deception well because it shows how wrong it can be to measure progress towards your goal: If your objective is freedom from the Chinese finger trap, then measuring progress by how close you are to freedom is exactly the wrong approach.

Maybe you think the Chinese finger trap is unfair. After all, it's designed to trick you. But the Chinese finger trap is actually a lot simpler than the kinds of problems we'd like to solve or the kinds of discoveries we'd like to make. The Chinese finger trap has only *one* deceptive stepping stone. There's almost no question that ambitious problems like designing artificial intelligence or curing cancer will require well more than a single deceptive stepping stone. In fact, the search space of any complex problem is sure to be *littered* with deceptive stepping stones.

Consider for example the game of chess: There are many moves that seem promising (such as capturing a piece) that later actually lead to trouble because of subtle unforeseen implications. As tricky as that makes chess, the world we live in is far more complicated than even that, so deception is going to be everywhere. The moral is that we can't expect to achieve anything great without overcoming some level of deception. And any problem without deception is trivial, because the stepping stones to solve it would be obvious. Clearly that is not the case for our most ambitious objectives, because we have yet to solve them. That's why deception is so universal. Puzzles like the Chinese finger trap will always exploit our mistaken assumptions, and even capturing the opponent's queen in chess can sometimes lead to a loss ten moves later. There will always be aliens leading to cars, just as vacuum tubes lead to computers and ragtime leads to rock and roll.

*   *   *

Deception is the key reason that objectives often don't work to drive achievement. If the objective is deceptive, as it must be for most ambitious problems, then setting it and guiding our efforts by it offers little help in reaching it. However, there is an alternative to focusing on objectives. If we go back to Picbreeder for a moment, one of the most interesting things about it is that it has no final objective. It's not aiming to discover some ultimate picture, the pinnacle of all pictures after which no other picture will ever be interesting. There's a better way to think of Picbreeder—as a *stepping-stone collector*. It collects stepping stones that create the potential to find even more stepping stones. Collecting stepping stones isn't like pursuing an objective because the stepping stones in the Picbreeder collection don't lead to somewhere in particular. Rather, they are the *road to everywhere*. To arrive somewhere remarkable we must be willing to hold many paths open without knowing where they might lead. Picbreeder shows that such a system is possible.

But Picbreeder is just one example of what you might call a *non-objective* system of discovery. There are some much more important processes that also work in this way. To name a couple very significant ones, natural evolution and human innovation also proceed without any final objective, as we'll see. Both of them are far more profound than Picbreeder, but it's still striking that they follow the same non-objective principle. However, the force of objective thinking is so powerful in our culture that we tend to think of both evolution and innovation as objectively driven. Right now you might even be questioning how we can claim that evolution or human innovation have no goals. But now that we have seen the strange dynamic of searching without objectives in Picbreeder, let's have a little fun by considering just how misleading objective thinking can be even for a process as familiar as evolution. Note that this kind of exploration will be a common theme throughout the rest of the book. In each case, we'll first show how the traditional objective-based view of discovery holds us back, and then we'll highlight how non-objective thinking can recast old assumptions in a whole new light. As the ultimate discovery process, it's fitting that we begin by revisiting evolution.

Natural evolution is a process of discovery and creation that produced an astronomical diversity of exceedingly complex organisms. Much of the natural world is a product of natural evolution, from the green carpet of life spanning the globe to our very selves. The intricacy and magnitude of its creations cannot be overstated; our own brains, themselves products of evolution, include 100 *trillion* neural connections, far exceeding the complexity of anything designed by engineers. Interestingly, it's popular to explain evolution as a process in which traits appear to satisfy some kind of global objective, portraying evolution only as a special sort of optimizer. However, like with Picbreeder, the truth is much deeper.

Let's try a thought experiment to see what happens when objective thinking is applied to natural evolution. You can think of this experiment as the ultimate high school biology laboratory challenge. Imagine that you're given an enormous Petri dish the size of Earth. On this Petri dish are placed single-celled organisms that are equivalent to the very first living cells on Earth, from which all other life eventually evolved. Your objective is to evolve organisms with human-level intelligence by *selecting which organisms should reproduce*. The basic idea is to replace natural selection with your own decisions about who gets to reproduce. For example, if you happen to spot what looks like the Einstein of amoebas, you can select it to reproduce and make more amoebas like it. Of course, it may sound difficult, but to make the problem easier you are allowed four billion years to finish.

The great thing about this experiment is that we know it's possible because those very single-celled organisms *did* evolve over billions of years into human beings. So it really should not be a problem because Earth is its own proof of what's possible. The main challenge is just to be a good breeder because selecting which organisms will reproduce is ultimately nothing more than animal breeding. All you need to do is select parents to mate that are increasingly human-like and voilà, you are done before you know it (well, at least after only a few billion years).

So what should be your strategy to breed single-celled organisms all the way to human-level intelligence? We'd like to suggest a clear-headed approach that gets right to the heart of the matter: You can administer intelligence tests to the single-celled organisms! Then all you need to do is pick the ones that score highest to be the parents of the next generation. Soon enough, we're on our way to a *real* Einstein, right?

Or maybe not. Clearly, this strategy is deeply flawed. If you really administered IQ tests to single-celled organisms, you would be lucky if they even survived, let alone evolved intelligence of any sort. But why wouldn't something like that work? After all, it respects the general principle that we measure progress towards our goals by comparing where we are to where we want to be. But that principle is increasingly suspicious, as this thought experiment exposes once again.

The problem is that the *stepping stones* to intelligence do not resemble intelligence at all. Put another way, human-level intelligence is a deceptive objective for evolution. Once again, deception rears its confusing and misdirecting head. Rather than increasing intelligence, the stepping stones that lead from single-celled organisms to humans include such unrelated innovations as multicellularity and bilateral symmetry. Millions of years ago our ancestor was a flatworm. It would not score any accolades for its intellect, but its one great achievement was bilateral symmetry. Who would ever think that bilateral symmetry is essential to writing poetry? But it was an essential stepping stone on the road to Shakespeare. The problem with the intelligence test approach is that it entirely fails to detect such monumentally important discoveries. Instead it wastes precious effort measuring a property that will not come into play in any important way until eons in the future. As philosopher Marshall McLuhan said, "I don't know who discovered water, but it wasn't a fish." Or in the words of the scientist Chuck Thacker, "You can't build railroads before it is railroad time." Neither should you administer intelligence tests to single-celled organisms if you want to evolve intelligence.

That may seem obvious because subjecting a cell to an IQ test (or any intelligence test) is unquestionably ridiculous. But the fact that it is ridiculous is exactly the point, and is why this experiment should ring alarm bells for anyone who still believes in the myth of the objective. Is it any less ridiculous to search for skulls on Picbreeder by comparing the image you're currently breeding to a skull? Is it any less ridiculous to try to achieve *any* far-off, ambitious objective by measuring how close it is to our best candidate so far? What this thought experiment exposes is that the traditional approach to achievement, driven by and informed by objectives, can lead to genuinely ridiculous behavior. But ridiculous or not, the assumption that objectives should drive achievement dominates our culture and our everyday lives.

Revisiting the Petri dish, how then *should* we actually approach this problem? If we can't pick parents for how closely they resemble the objective, then what alternative is there? Well obviously there is an alternative, because human-level intelligence *did* evolve. But evolution in nature wasn't administering IQ tests to cells floating in a chemical soup. Here there is again a strong analogy with Picbreeder. Evolution on Earth was *not* trying to evolve human-level intelligence. And that is the only reason *it did*. In other words, the only way such an incredible outcome as the hundred-trillion-connection human brain can be achieved over billions of years of epic progress is by *not* setting it as the objective. Just as Ken could only evolve the Picbreeder *Car* by not trying to evolve a car, so could nature only produce *us* by not trying to evolve us.

Like Picbreeder, evolution in nature is a stepping-stone collector. These stepping stones are collected not because they may lead to some far off primary objective, some ultimate uber-organism towards which all of life is directed, but because they are well-adapted in their own right. Each organism on the path to humans reproduced because it was successful in its own niche at its own time. Flatworms squirmed about with their newly-discovered symmetric bodies and were able to survive and reproduce, the only requirement for continuing a lineage in evolution. Whether or not some distant descendant would be human had nothing to do with it. In that sense, what nature ultimately produced was not its objective, and—like Picbreeder—that's why it produced so many remarkable things.

*   *   *

Consider how many goals of engineering are inspired by the products of evolution, even though none of them were the objective of evolution. For example, the flight of birds inspires air travel, but no one ever chose to reward the distant ancestors of birds simply because they might lead to birds. Photosynthesis inspires solar power, but plants didn't evolve because they were someone's objective. Even the human mind inspires research in artificial intelligence, but as our thought experiment showed, it would be foolish to begin evolution with the sole objective of producing human intelligence. The bottom line is that many of our greatest engineering aspirations—such as flight, solar power, artificial intelligence—were not the explicit objective of evolution, though it created all of them. It created them because nature is a stepping-stone collector, accumulating steps towards ever-more complicated novelties, marching onward onto the mist-cloaked lake of possible life-forms, heading eternally both everywhere and nowhere in particular. That's the signature, now increasingly familiar, of processes that produce amazing innovations.

Even so, it's common to believe that evolution does have an objective, which is *to survive and reproduce*. This story of survival and reproduction is popular and supports the cultural assumption that all great achievements are driven by objectives. But we should be careful when objective tales are spun around open-ended constraints like "survive and reproduce," because meeting a constraint is much different from what is usually *meant* by objective-driven achievement.

For example, how often is the *product* of an objective-driven effort not the objective? Birds are a product of evolution but birds were not the objective. Nowhere in *survive and reproduce* does it say anything about birds. Would any entrepreneur start a company with the sole objective of creating a product that *lasts a long time*? And even if they did, how strange would it then be if they ended up building an airplane? We would hardly regard such a scenario as a normal business plan, let alone a sane one. Usually, the objective is a well-defined product that you ultimately do produce if you are successful, not a nebulous generality.

That's not the only difference between *survive and reproduce* and the usual sense of objectives. Usually, when we formulate an ambitious objective, we haven't *already* achieved the very objective that we're setting. That would be a rather odd way to start. What kind of strange marathon is over exactly when it begins? But that is precisely how *survive and reproduce* works: Clearly the very first organism on Earth survived and reproduced, or we wouldn't be here. Not only that, but then so did every other organism from the very beginning in the direct chain through the tree of life that leads to us. So we have this incredible chain of successful survivors and reproducers, each one satisfying the very same objective over and over again. Is that really objective-driven discovery in the traditional sense?

Perhaps *survive and reproduce* can be more naturally seen as a *constraint* on evolution. In other words, it's a kind of *minimal criterion* that all creatures must satisfy to continue evolving. But it describes nothing about the products that might be created, nothing about the difference between where we are today and where we might be tomorrow, and nothing about the potential for greatness lurking behind it. And by viewing survival in nature as a constraint rather than as an objective we no longer have to bend words in unnatural ways.

Of course *survive and reproduce* is an important constraint (and it is discussed in more detail following the book's conclusion in the first case study), but it's not the kind of objective we ordinarily seek. If you want to design a car then your objective is generally to design a car. Constraints like *survive and reproduce* are something else—they are part of the alternative, in which we let go of defined objectives and instead explore the stepping stones. *Survive and reproduce* is a means to finding stepping stones—it allows evolution to identify successful organisms that may lead to other successful organisms, nothing less and nothing more. But it's not the only means to non-objective exploration. In fact, neither is evolution the only example in our world of such a process. Human innovation, taken as a whole, also works that way.

$$*   *   *$$

With human innovation in mind, let's try another thought experiment. Computers were only invented in the last century, but what if instead the first computer had been invented 5,000 years ago? Imagine how powerful the Internet would then be today! So let's try to give the whole thing a head start by traveling back in time 5,000 years and gathering all the most brilliant minds of the day. We'll bring all of them together in a far-off retreat, like a prehistoric Manhattan Project, and suggest to them the idea of this wonderful programmable machine. In other words, their objective will be to build a computer, 5,000 years ago.

The interesting question is whether this project makes any sense. The hope would be that committing the era's top minds to achieve this highly ambitious objective would be worth pulling them away from other more immediate concerns. In this sense, it makes a good analogy with similarly ambitious objectives in which we might invest today. Unfortunately though, it will not turn out well—we might as well be asking them to build a time machine.

The fundamental problem is that 5,000 years ago the stepping stones to efficient computers were not yet uncovered. So no matter how brilliant our team, they couldn't possibly anticipate and develop the intermediate stepping stones necessary to assemble the final product. For example, as noted in Chap. 1, the vacuum tube is a fundamental stepping stone to early computers, but the *idea* of computation provides no clue to the need for vacuum tubes, or to the need for electricity for that matter. You might counter that given enough time they might muddle through the problem to arrive at vacuum tubes. But history doesn't suggest such an outcome because the inventors of vacuum tubes were explicitly *not* thinking of computation. In fact, it's much more likely that you will think of vacuum tubes if you're interested in electrical experiments, not computation.

Once again the objective is deceptive, diverting us from the right trail. The best way to get computation is not to force great minds to waste their lives pondering a distant dream, but to let the great minds pursue their own interests in their present reality. Some will go in a direction that centuries later might lead to computation, and some will go in other directions, but at least they will be marching forward, stepping stone by stepping stone, which is ultimately the only realistic path to the future.

In fact, the computer-building thought experiment can easily be applied to nearly *any* other invention. Because most interesting inventions are simply the most recent fruits of chains of ideas spanning centuries, they too will necessarily depend upon a prior invention created for an entirely different purpose. In fact, stretching this line of thinking to its logical conclusion leads to a provocative hypothesis about invention in general: *Almost no prerequisite to any major invention was invented with that invention in mind.* While this idea sounds strange, if it's even partially true then its implications for objective-driven innovation are sobering. After all, what hope is there of achieving ambitious objectives if their prerequisites are almost sure to come from someone with an entirely different objective? But there is good reason to believe that the world works exactly in this way. Electricity was not discovered with computation in mind, or even with vacuum tubes in mind, and neither were vacuum tubes invented to foster building computers. We simply lack the foresight to comprehend what one discovery will later make possible.

Often the stories we tell about great inventions gloss over this less romantic aspect. We hear tales of geniuses like the Wright brothers who invented machines that could fly, these can-do achievers who strived heroically against all odds to change the world forever. And of course they deserve the credit for their achievement, following generations of failed attempts, to finally build a winged machine that can fly. But the Wright brothers can't claim credit for the endless chain of human innovation that precedes them. That chain includes the gas-powered reciprocating internal combustion engine, an essential component of the first airplane, which—not surprisingly by now—was not first invented with flight in mind [39].

Rather, it was the engine behind early three-wheeled automobiles and later factory applications like printing presses, water pumps, and machine tools. The modern internal combustion engine itself was preceded by the induction coil, which similarly was not invented with engines in mind [40]. Rather, it aided early electrical experiments as a convenient high-voltage trigger. Its use in the "Crookes tube" (an early experimental setup involving a crude partial vacuum in a glass tube with two electrodes across which a spark could travel) led to the discovery of cathode rays (i.e. electrons) and later the discovery of X-rays. As usual, each link in the chain of innovations, from induction coil to internal combustion engine to airplane, was not invented with the next link in mind. The future that the past created was *not* the vision of the past, but instead what the past unexpectedly enabled.

The genius of the Wright brothers wasn't to invent every necessary component for flight from scratch, but to recognize that we were only a stepping stone away from flight given past innovations. Great invention is defined by the realization that the prerequisites are in place, laid before us by predecessors with entirely unrelated ambitions, just waiting to be combined and enhanced. The flash of insight is seeing the bridge to the next stepping stone by building from the old ones. And the story of those stepping stones is not a story of intentional objective-driven building, one piece at a time towards some distant über-invention as conceived by an overarching plan. On the contrary, just like in natural evolution and just like in Picbreeder, the stepping stones are laid in their own context for their own independent reasons, not because a visionary foresaw their role in future greatness. Just as nature and Picbreeder are both stepping-stone collectors, so is the tree of human innovation, growing ever-outward, towards computers, Internet, cars, and planes—everywhere you might want to go and at the same time paradoxically nowhere in particular.

These examples highlight that Picbreeder is not some abnormal curiosity. In reality, Picbreeder is just one example of a fascinating class of phenomena that we might call *non-objective search processes*, or perhaps *stepping stone collectors*. The prolific creativity of these kinds of processes is difficult to overstate. After all, these are the same processes that created *us*, and through which we conquered the skies and networked the world. Non-objective search is the true source of much that gives value to our lives. When we unleash search from the trap of the objective, liberating it from the requirement to move only towards where we hope to arrive, it becomes a kind of treasure-hunter that finds needles in the haystack of what's possible. So then why are so many of our efforts still dominated by the mythical objective? Whatever your goals are, from finding the perfect partner to creating the next great invention, when objectives are ambitious, the only reward you're likely to receive is deception. That's what you get for traveling by the false compass.

*   *   *

Even if your goals aren't particularly noble, you can't avoid the problem of deception. Maybe you just want to become rich. But as we saw from the personal stories in the last chapter, measuring success against the objective is likely to lead you on the wrong path in all sorts of situations. Deception applies to becoming rich just as everywhere else. For example, what sense would it make to decline an unpaid internship doing something you love simply because it doesn't make you any more rich? In fact, if you do become rich, it's probably because you *did* pursue your passion, not because you pursued money per se. Passion is what drives you to that point, and then one day you might realize that you are only one stepping stone away from being rich. And *that* is the moment, when you are one stepping stone away, when you make the move you need to make and become rich. But becoming rich didn't guide every life decision up to that point. On the contrary, a single-minded preoccupation with money is likely exactly the wrong road to abundant wealth.

It's important to understand that this lesson is not a lecture on morality, at least in the context of this book. Instead, it's exactly the same lesson we see in nature, the same we see in human innovation, and the same we see in Picbreeder. The stepping stones don't resemble the final destination. It has nothing to do with right and wrong. It has to do with search.

We should be concerned by the disconnect between how the world is *supposed to work* and the way it *really does work*. When we set out to achieve our dreams, we're supposed to know what our dreams are, and to strive for them with passion and commitment. But this philosophy leads to absurdities if taken literally. You can't evolve intelligence in a Petri dish based on measuring intelligence. You can't build a computer simply through determination and intellect—you need the stepping stones. You can't become rich simply by seeking a higher salary—getting a raise today doesn't guarantee another raise will ever come in the future. There's much we cannot achieve by trying to achieve it.

While these various thought experiments test the extremes, that doesn't mean they can be easily dismissed. It would be one thing simply to say that certain objectives are impossible, but that's not the message here because all these astonishing achievements actually *did* occur. What should really worry us is that they all occurred without explicit objectives. Human intelligence *did* evolve, but it was never set as an explicit objective for evolution. Computers *were* invented, though their prerequisites were not invented with computation in mind. Many people *do* become rich, not because they decided to become rich, but because they pursued their passion, which happened to lead to a lot of money. And of course the *Car* on Picbreeder *was* evolved, even though its discoverer was not looking for a car. All of this is not only possible but actually came to pass. But it's only when the objective is ignored, when the reigns of exploration swing free, that the farthest frontiers are conquered.

Maybe after all that you're still a fan of objectives. So it's important to recall that the concern here is with *ambitious* objectives—if they are only a stepping stone away, then setting and following objectives still makes good sense. The problem is that the ambitious objectives are the interesting ones, and the idea that the best way to achieve them is by ignoring them flies in the face of common intuition and conventional wisdom. More deeply it suggests that *something is wrong at the heart of search*. It just doesn't seem to work like it's supposed to. The world's greatest compass can get us lost while a mysterious form of ignorance turns out to be surprisingly powerful. Whenever evidence begins to threaten established wisdom, of course it's natural to hesitate. Human nature doesn't abandon convention without a fight. But while one response is to try to argue for normalcy and the status quo, the positive side of uncertainty is *opportunity*. If the world doesn't work the way we thought it should, then perhaps the way it really works can be seized to our advantage. To explore this opportunity, the next chapter turns to the question of how to play the game of discovery on its own terms, without our trusted compass: untamed, wild, and unfamiliar.

Chapter 5
The Interesting and the Novel

> *Seize from every moment its unique novelty and do not prepare your joys.*
>
> Andre Gide

We've all probably met the guy who resolves on New Year's day to learn fluent Mandarin, run seven miles a day, and eat only carrots and apples for three months. Then a week later in January nobody's surprised when it's all forgotten. You may not need to see a survey to be convinced that New Year's resolutions often don't stick, but just for the record, although over half of the people who make such resolutions think they'll succeed, only 12 % actually do [41].

That kind of dismal statistic is a reminder that setting objectives, while appealing in the moment, is the easy part. It doesn't take much effort to state what you want to be, where you want to go, or what you want to accomplish. The problem is getting there. More specifically, the problem is that it's hard to identify the stepping stones between here and the objective. This insight suggests a strange idea: Perhaps the effort invested in specifying clear objectives would be sometimes better spent in identifying promising stepping stones, but *not* specifically those leading to the objective. After all, the objective offers few clues to what its stepping stones should be. So maybe there's a different way to think about search. Instead of worrying about *where we want to be*, we could compare where we are now to *where we have been*. If we find ourselves somewhere genuinely novel, then this novel discovery may later prove a stepping stone to new frontiers. While we may not know what those frontiers are, the present stepping stone becomes the gateway to finding out.

Our preoccupation with objectives is really a preoccupation with the future. Every moment ends up measured against where we want to be in the future. Are we creeping closer to our goal? Does the assessment confirm that we're moving forward? The future becomes a distant beacon by which all endeavors are lit. But this beacon is too often deceptive, playing tricks with the light that lead us astray: The beacon of air travel says nothing of induction coils and the beacon of computation says nothing of vacuum tubes. Even so, long ago we visited those very stepping stones entirely unaware that they might lead to such distant horizons.

© Springer International Publishing Switzerland 2015
K.O. Stanley, J. Lehman, *Why Greatness Cannot Be Planned*,
DOI 10.1007/978-3-319-15524-1_5

What good then is it to compare the present with the idealized future? Let's instead try something different and more principled. We can instead compare to the *past*, which is a lot easier than the future because we know it—the past already happened.

The past doesn't tell us about the objective but it does offer a clue to something equally if not more important—the past is a guide to *novelty*. But unlike the future, there's no ambiguity and no deception because we actually know where we were in the past, so we know how it compares to where we are today. Instead of judging our progress towards a goal, the past allows us to judge our liberation from the outdated. Interestingly, the question then changes from what we're approaching to what we're escaping. And the exciting thing about escaping the past is that it opens new possibilities.

The point is that *novelty* can often act as a stepping stone detector because anything novel is a potential stepping stone to something even more novel. In other words, novelty is a rough shortcut for identifying *interestingness*: Interesting ideas are those that open up new possibilities. And while it might sound wishy-washy to go looking for "interesting" things, interestingness is a surprisingly deep and important concept. In the words of the famous philosopher Alfred Whitehead [42]: "It is more important that a proposition be interesting than it be true." W.T. Stace [43], another philosopher, adds that "the criticism that interestingness is a trivial end proceeds from a scale of values thus perverted and turned upside down." Far from trivial, novel and interesting ideas tend to suggest new ways of thinking that lead to further novelties.

The important point is that novelty (and interestingness) can compound over time by continually making new things possible. So instead of seeking a final objective, by looking for novelty the reward is an endless chain of stepping stones branching out into the future as novelty leads to further novelty. Rather than thinking of the future as a *destination*, it becomes a road, a path of undefined potential. This non-objective perspective captures better the spirit of processes like Picbreeder, evolution in nature, and human innovation—ratcheting processes that build stepping stone upon stepping stone, branching and *diverging* ever outward to everywhere and nowhere in particular.

In Picbreeder, the *Alien Face* was not chosen because it might lead to the *Car*, but because the *Alien Face* itself was something interesting and novel. It was worth exploring the path opened by the *Alien Face* because it held *potential*—not the kind of objective potential measured by an intelligence test or performance assessment— but the potential that hangs in the sunset viewed over an endless sea, the transcendent possibility of an open future. Let's try to capture *that* kind of potential in a bottle. The key to it will be chasing novelty.

But there might still seem to be a problem. Chasing novelty suggests a kind of aimless uncertainty. How do we know where we're going? But that's exactly the point. The greatest processes of innovation work precisely because they are *not* trying to go anywhere in particular. In this sense, we've abandoned the false security of the objective to embrace the wild possibility of the unknown. Of course, there's still reason for concern. Such a search for novelty still feels unanchored and perhaps even almost *random*. Would it not simply chart a course from one fleeting novelty to another? Why should we believe that such a process has any *meaning* to it?

It's natural to fear that hunting for novelty might not lead to anything meaningful. One of the main reasons for this kind of doubt has to do with *information*. The fear is that the only useful information for guiding search is the kind obtained through considering what you hope to find. But the truth is that novelty is no less information-rich than the concept of the objective. It's just *different* information. In fact, the argument can be made that the information driving the concept of novelty is actually more plentiful and reliable than that provided by the objective, especially when you consider that the objective is often a false compass. Rather than relying on a false compass, novelty only asks us to compare where we are with where we've been.

In short, objectives mean sailing to a distant destination with an unknown path while novelty requires only steering away from where we've been already. Deviating from the past is simpler and richer with information because we can look at the whole history of past discoveries to inform our judgment of current novelty. So it's not unreasonable to believe that novelty is a meaningful engine for progress.

Another clue to the importance of novelty in innovation is that humans tend to be very sensitive to it. Often we feel the urge to explore a particular path or idea despite being unsure where it might lead. Our intuitions and hunches often prod us in directions that might not be justified objectively but still lead to something different or interesting. So it's no coincidence that the concept of *interestingness* comes up naturally when discussing novelty. When an idea feels genuinely novel, that's often enough to make us curious. The idea interests us even if its ultimate purpose is unclear.

This insight connects to another common myth about achievement. This *myth of serendipity* is that serendipity is an accident. The classic stereotype for serendipitous discovery is the mad scientist stumbling clumsily into some profound breakthrough. It brings to mind a cartoonish character accidentally exploding a bottle of peanut butter in a microwave oven only to discover the secret to anti-gravity. But this kind of caricature undeservedly gives serendipity a bad name because it's so rarely a bumbling accident.

The reality is that we humans have a nose for the interesting. We understand that if we take the interesting path, it may yet lead somewhere important, even though we might not know where. The history of serendipitous discovery supports this idea. If serendipitous discovery was simply accidental, then it wouldn't take any particular special education or intellect to make such discoveries. For all we know, being a little disorganized or crazy might even be the best way to start. But that doesn't seem to be the case in the real world because most major serendipitous discoverers are not fueled by crazy ideas. In fact, most are intelligent, educated, and accomplished.

For instance, Isaac Newton's chance observation of an apple falling from a tree led to his discovery of the universal law of gravitation [44]. But Newton's career wasn't all about apples falling from trees—he made many additional great discoveries in mathematics, astronomy, and physics. Another example is the French scientist Louis Pasteur, who significantly contributed to the field of chemistry and is also one of the founders of microbiology. Many of his important findings were seemingly accidental, including the discovery of "chiral" molecules (i.e. molecules that come in mirror image forms with different properties) or the life-saving process for creating bacterial vaccines [45]. But like Newton he was consistently able to innovate across multiple disciplines. There's no shortage of these kinds of stories. After realizing one day while bathing that the water his body displaced in the bathtub was equal to its volume, the ancient Greek mathematician Archimedes had his infamous "eureka" moment and rushed naked through the streets [45]. But we remember Archimedes more for a string of fundamental innovations such as the lever, the "Archimedes screw," and the law of hydrostatics. These were not crazy, uneducated men who were simply lucky.

Behind any serendipitous discovery there's nearly always an open-minded thinker with a strong gut feeling for what plan will yield the most interesting results. While the law of gravity hid in plain sight for thousands of years, Newton was the first to uncover it. As William Whewell wrote: "Thousands of men, even of the most inquiring and speculative men, had seen bodies fall; but who, except Newton, ever followed the accident to such consequences [46]?" It was not just mere chance that these discoverers noticed something profound. As Louis Pasteur himself once famously said: "In the fields of observation chance favors only the prepared mind [47]."

The question is, if serendipitous discovery really isn't such an accident, can it result from searching for novelty and interestingness—even without a specific objective in mind? If so, it should be possible to show scientifically that this kind of serendipitous approach works. At least there should be an experiment we could perform that would provide some evidence for the idea. And as it turns out, it's actually possible to run such an experiment, but you have to prepare yourself for an unusual procedure: To investigate how promising it is to search without objectives, we'll design a kind of computer program, or *algorithm*, that has no objective.

*   *   *

At first glance, a computer algorithm without an objective may seem like a contradiction. The word "algorithm" brings to mind something directed and mechanical, and algorithms are typically recipes for solving particular problems. There are various objective-driven algorithms that mechanically achieve tasks such as solving differential equations, sorting large lists, and encrypting data. But at its heart the idea of an algorithm is more general. It's a way of clearly describing a process, a recipe so unambiguous that a computer can follow it. So while most algorithms do have objectives, they can just as easily describe processes without objectives—like searching for novelty. And because algorithms can be expressed concretely as computer programs that can be analyzed and studied, they can help us test scientific hypotheses.

The main advantage of writing an algorithm without an objective is that we can put our money where our mouth is: If searching for novelty alone really works for making useful discoveries, then it should be possible literally to formalize that process as an algorithm. Once that's done, it can actually be tested. In the field of

AI (unlike, for example, in the field of psychology) this philosophy of building an algorithm to test a theory is fully embraced. In fact, in AI research no explanation is considered good enough unless it is built as a computer program and then run on a computer to test it. In that way, AI has a demanding threshold for success because its researchers can't simply offer explanations, but must actually build a prototype of their theory and show that it works. So in this case we can borrow this philosophy and apply it to non-objective search: Let's see what happened when we programmed a computer to search only for novelty with no specific objective.

The new algorithm that we programmed is called *novelty search*. It was initially inspired by observing people playing with Picbreeder. We noticed that Picbreeder users make their best discoveries if those discoveries aren't their objective. These successful users were instead following their instinct towards the interesting and novel. This realization is what led to trying to program a computer to do the same type of thing. And one nice consequence of programming an idea as an algorithm is that it forces us to be clear about what it really means. In other words, there's no way to hide behind fuzzy words when a machine is running the tests. So to make an algorithm we need to decide how exactly a computer should search for novelty.

The first step towards testing such a program is to decide on what's called the *domain*. In other words, the computer only searches for novelty within a particular category, such as novel art, novel music, or novel robot behaviors. The reason for making such a decision is that each domain might need to be programmed in a different way. But the important outcome is that the domain defines the space that's being explored by the algorithm.

To make the idea easier to understand, consider for a moment the space of *behaviors*. Most computer experiments with novelty search have focused on this space. Usually in novelty search the term "behavior" refers to the sequence of actions taken by a real or simulated robot. More simply, a robot's behavior is what it does when placed in a particular situation. Recall the endless room of pictures that we used to visualize the space of all possible images in Chap. 1. We can imagine a similar sprawling hall of robot behaviors, where one corner might contain robots that do nothing but turn in circles, while within another corner robots might be tracing the outline of the Mona Lisa on the floor. It's easy to see how some behaviors in this great hall are very different than others. For example, a robot that crashes into a wall is much different than one that navigates down a hallway and then enters a door. Once we have a way to tell how behaviors can be different it becomes possible to ask what is novel.

Trying to find novel behaviors can help to illustrate how searching for novelty leads to to interesting results even if there is no specific objective. Imagine that a robot is released at one end of a hallway with an open door at the other end. This sort of experiment is common in the field of machine learning, which attempts to give computers the ability to learn from experience. In a typical experiment of this type, the robot would learn to approach the doorway by becoming increasingly skilled at navigating the hallway. For example, over a series of trials in which the robot is always put back at its starting position, it might come increasingly close to crossing the entire hallway, which is the objective. In this objective-driven approach, whichever behavior leads the robot closest to the open doorway would then become the stepping stone for attempting new behaviors. This view of progress as a series of incremental improvements that gradually approach the objective reflects the usual way achievement is pursued in our culture.

But the task can also be solved in a much different way based on novelty search: Instead of attempting to make it to the other side of the hallway, the robot can simply try to do something different than it has done in the past. As illustrated in Fig. 5.1, the robot might first crash into a wall because initially it's not experienced at navigating hallways. However, unlike when it's pursuing an objective, in novelty search the robot's crash is considered *good* because we've never seen it do that before. In other words, the behavior is novel, which is what we care about when searching for novelty. But if crashing into a wall is good, what would the robot do next?

The answer is that it might crash into a different wall, but once again as long as it's *different* from the first crash, it's also going to be considered good. Even if the second crash is *farther* from the goal than the first, it's still considered a good sign in

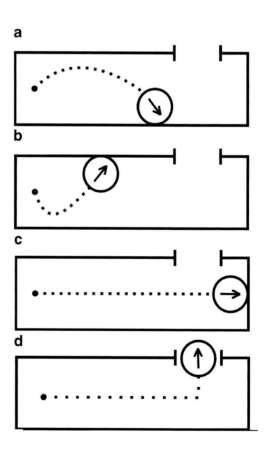

Fig. 5.1 A series of novel behaviors. By exhausting the various ways to crash, a search for novelty can increase its understanding of navigating corridors, which eventually allows it to discover how to exit through the door even though exiting was not the objective of the search.

the pursuit of novelty because it's a different crash. As you can see, this attitude of appreciating novel situations without being judgmental already makes the novelty search different from an objective-driven pursuit.

Crashing into various walls may not sound that exciting, but what happens next is magical and highlights the power of novelty search. At some point, after crashing into enough walls, there are no more new walls to crash into. At that moment, novelty search has exhausted all the options for crashing and a remarkable fact comes into play: The only way for the robot to do something novel is now by *not crashing*. This advance is interesting because learning to avoid walls was never expressed as an objective. But even though it wasn't the objective, the robot seeking only novelty eventually must learn to avoid walls *anyway* to have the hope of continuing to produce novel behaviors.

In fact, eventually the novelty-seeking robot will even have to enter the doorway on the far side because once again it will exhaust all the possibilities for novel behaviors that remain within the same hallway. The result is something very strange: A robot told only to seek novelty eventually learns how to avoid walls, navigate a hallway, and enter doors even though none of those are ever actually requested or rewarded as objectives. Following this logic, a push towards novelty seems to produce more sophistication than you might expect.

At the same time, it might seem that this apparent success is simply a result of "trying everything" (which computer scientists call *exhaustive enumeration*). If you really have the time to try every behavior under the sun, eventually you'll end up doing something that seems intelligent, but it might take you almost forever to get to it. That doesn't sound like a smart approach, and it turns out that discovery in novelty search is deeper than simply trying every behavior you can think of. The reason it's more interesting than that is that novelty search tends to produce behaviors in a certain *order*.

Order is a critical factor in search and discovery. In fact, the main reason we have faith in any kind of search is that we expect it to encounter stepping stones in a certain sensible order. For objective-driven search, what we usually expect is *bad behavior before good behavior*. In other words, we expect the quality of the behaviors to improve over the course of the search. In that way, the objective leads to a succession of discoveries that seems to make sense.

The problem is that the order from bad to good, while attractive, is unfortunately naive. It's just another road to the same tired formula for objective-driven deception. Recall the Chinese finger trap—there, the only order that leads to success is from bad to *worse* before getting better. All deceptive problems will at some point (and often at many points) along the trail exhibit this misleading property. So if you take into account the problem of deception, following an order only from bad to good should hardly build confidence. It's as naive as believing that single-celled organisms can be bred into Einsteins through IQ tests (and in fact in Chap. 7 we will see that trying to improve only from bad to good has surprising implications for student testing as well). These failings mean that we can stop worrying about always moving from worse to better and consider less obvious orderings that might actually be more promising in reality.

As you might expect, novelty search leads to one of these different orderings. It doesn't search from bad to good because without an objective it doesn't even know what "good" is. Although it might appear that being more novel is "better" than being less novel, it all depends on what you've seen so far—someone else with different experiences might come up with exactly the opposite judgment. When rewarding novelty, "better" doesn't stay "better" over time. The reason is that as soon as a novel behavior is discovered, it quickly becomes *less novel* as similar behaviors are discovered.

The point is that what is considered novel depends completely upon time and context. In fact, before the search begins we can't even say which behaviors are more or less novel because novelty is a *relative* measure. That's why considering novelty in isolation makes no sense—how new something is depends on what's been seen before.

Objective-driven search is much different: A car with a more efficient engine is *always* more efficient than a car with a less efficient engine, no matter when either of them was invented. The point is that what's better and what's worse doesn't change when searching for an objective. Because novelty search can't provide such a consistent notion of bad and good, it also can't provide an ordering from bad to good. But it does in fact provide a more interesting ordering: from *simple to complex*.

While most people are familiar with thinking of progress as a journey from worse to better, a journey from simplicity to complexity without a clear destination is more exotic. But in a way it's also more sensible because it's not subject to deception (because you're not trying to get anywhere in particular). The reason that searching for novelty leads from simplicity to complexity is itself surprisingly straightforward: When all the simple ways to behave are exhausted, the *only* new behaviors that remain to discover are more complex. For example, consider again the robot in the hallway. At first virtually any behavior is novel because the robot has never tried anything before. And most often those very first behaviors will tend to be simple, just as simple inventions are stepping stones to more complex inventions.

An example of such a simple behavior is always running forward, even directly into a wall. But what really makes a behavior "simple?" There's much that could be said about the nature of simplicity, but for our purposes the key is that it requires no *information* or *knowledge* about the world. Running into a wall is easy because you can do it without knowing anything about walls, hallways, and in fact without the ability to perceive anything whatsoever: The robot's forward motor is simply turned on and it barrels ahead unconditionally, oblivious to its environment. But eventually to navigate a hallway with walls and *not* crash into them will require acquiring some knowledge about walls. That new knowledge is the *magic step* when a novelty search climbs out of ignorance into meaning. Eventually doing something genuinely novel always requires learning something about the world. You can't invent a new dance without first knowing how to walk, and you can't walk without some understanding (at least subconscious) of gravity and motion.

In fact, this is an important insight: Because eventually you have to acquire some kind of knowledge to continue to produce novelty, it means that novelty search is a kind of *information accumulator* about the world in which it takes place. The longer the search progresses, the more information about the world it ends up accumulating. And of course information and complexity go hand in hand—more complex behaviors require more information.

Interestingly, novelty search is not the only kind of search that accumulates information. Information accumulation and increasing complexity are the tell-tale signs of *any* kind of search without an explicit objective. Novelty search is a special kind of non-objective search, but others, such as natural evolution, clearly exhibit this signature dynamic as well. While natural evolution is different from novelty search (their relation will be explored in greater depth in the first case study), it shares with novelty search the key property that what it ultimately produces is not its objective. For that reason again, natural evolution also becomes a simple-to-complex information accumulator.

As Stephen Jay Gould has pointed out in evolution, once all the simple ways to live are exhausted, the only way to create a new species or niche is to become more complex [48]. In other words, there are only so many ways of being a bacteria. That's why increasing complexity is almost inevitable if evolution is to continue. But these increases in complexity are not arbitrary. Rather, they reflect the properties of the world in which evolution takes place: Eyes represent the presence of light in the universe. Ears signify mechanical vibration. Legs are reflections of gravity, and lungs of oxygen.

In the usual interpretation of evolution, innovations like eyes or lungs might be considered objective improvements, increasing a creature's ability to survive. But they can also be viewed as the inevitable tendency of a search with no final objective to accumulate information about its world. After all, there was nothing particularly *wrong* with the original single-celled organisms that possessed none of these fancy additions. They were surviving just fine. The only problem was that to do something new required reflecting some aspect of the natural world back into the DNA. Sight-driven behavior isn't strictly *necessary*—it's just that if you keep trying new designs through mutation, even though there's no objective, eventually you will hit upon the fact that light exists. Then it will become a part of evolution's accumulated inventory of information.

In a sense, over eons our bodies have become a kind of encyclopedia of facts about the universe in which they exist. Not only are many physical aspects of reality reflected in our bodies' structure (for example, light, sound, gravity, heat, air, etc.), but evolution has continued for so long that we now actually encode incredibly specific details of the universe somewhere within us: Our brains remember which planets revolve around the sun and even the price of a bagel at the corner shop. The ability to learn and adapt over our lifetime has propelled the evolutionary information accumulator to a recent extreme. Of course, that doesn't mean the process will stop with us. But what we observe again is that a search without a clear objective (evolution in this case) accumulates information as it moves from the most simple single-celled organisms to the most complex animals. That's why the creatures of Earth have become a kind of mirror held up to the world that reflects back in tremendous diversity the physical possibilities enabled by our universe.

This view of non-objective search also explains the fact that Picbreeder is a mirror reflecting back at us something about the world of humans. After all, humans *are* the world through which Picbreeder progresses. So it's no surprise that Picbreeder has become a catalog of familiar themes from butterflies to faces, from castles to planets, from sunsets to spaceships. None of these were its objective, but they are all being discovered.

Like Picbreeder or natural evolution, novelty search is another kind of non-objective search. It's not as fantastic as natural evolution, but the good thing about it is that it can be turned into an algorithm that runs on a computer, so we get to test it scientifically and see what it does. It's also convenient because it can be applied to easily-programmed domains like simple simulations of robots inside of hallways, just as you can imagine that the computer game "Pong" requires less effort to write than a fully-immersive modern three-dimensional shooter game (which often cost millions of dollars to develop). So to see the benefits of searching without an objective in novelty search we don't have to write the most complicated of programs—one that captures the Earth in all its glory—as might be necessary to recreate something like natural evolution. And if it works as expected, we should be able to spot the tell-tale non-objective signs of the simple-to-complex information accumulator when novelty search runs. For novelties to be continually found, eventually the robot would have to discover that the world is made of walls and doors, and that robots crash into walls but fit through doorways.

But even if you buy the argument so far about the order of the search from simple to complex, you may still be worried that novelty search will end up wandering forever through meaningless behaviors. One reason objectives are reassuring is that they can filter an overwhelming space of possibilities to only a few practical options. For example, before driving to work nobody seriously considers the merits of crawling there instead. In other words, objectives can weed out clearly inferior ideas, which could eliminate pointless effort we might otherwise invest in irrelevant activities. In contrast, novelty search seems to lack this kind of practical constraint, which might mean it would waste a lot of time meandering through a space of meaningless possibilities.

However, there's a good reason to believe that we don't need the constraint of the objective to avoid meaninglessness: The world provides its own constraints. Many behaviors that are possible to imagine (like flying) would not be considered by novelty search because they're *impossible*. For example, a robot can't walk through a wall, so even though we can imagine behaviors that involve teleportation, none of them would be considered because that area of the search space doesn't exist: Teleportation is physically impossible.

In general, many behaviors that we can *imagine* collapse to the same *actual* behavior in reality. There may be thousands of different imaginable behaviors that attempt walking through walls, but because of physics all of them are reduced to the same behavior in reality of crashing into a wall and stopping. You simply can't walk through a wall. Gravity constrains our own behaviors in a similar way, so no matter how you imagine flying unaided through the sky when you jump off your front porch, in reality it will always end with bruises caused by the same unfortunate collision with the ground.

So the space of behaviors that are actually attempted while searching for novelty is a tiny part of the much larger space of *all behaviors that we can imagine*, which helps make it practical. This idea that the physics of the world limits the behaviors considered by novelty search also explains its tendency to accumulate information about the world: The behaviors that really become stepping stones to further behaviors are the ones that *respect how the world actually works*. Driving to work leads to more possibilities for novelty than crawling there, because your entire day isn't consumed by traveling to and from your job. So given both options, a search for novelty would tend to focus on driving to work rather than crawling because it's a better stepping stone. It's for this reason that further exploration ends up focusing on concepts that make sense. In short, the best way to create novelty is to exploit the way the world really works and accumulate information about it.

At this point you might question whether novelty is some kind of special objective. In fact, we've heard this question a lot over the years since the novelty search algorithm was first introduced in 2008. It's common to be a little skeptical about the counterintuitive message that discovery works better without objectives. Whenever a new theory challenges the dominant worldview, it's natural to seek to reestablish the original order. One way to do that is to *reinterpret* the new theory to fit the old way of thinking, to avoid having to start all over again. In this spirit, the most popular attempt to rescue the objective-driven paradigm is to try to force novelty *back into it* by saying that novelty is itself an objective. But there are significant downsides to this tactic. As we review some of these arguments next, you might be reminded of the discussion from the previous chapter on why *survive and reproduce* isn't a traditional objective. But the difference here is that we're concerned with the broader issue of whether *novelty* itself should be called an objective.

With traditional objectives, success means reaching your objective. For example, if you wanted to become a banker and then became a banker, then your objective is fulfilled. When we think of objectives, we usually assume that our objective is satisfied when we achieve what we set out to achieve. But—here's the first problem with calling novelty an objective—novelty doesn't work that way. After all, you might also become a banker if you set out to act differently than other people (or differently than you have in the past), but in that case *becoming a banker* was *not* your objective. With novelty, what you become or what you achieve is never your objective. So there's something different about novelty.

You still might object that even if you did somehow become a banker by trying to be novel, you still fulfilled your objective of *being novel*, even if being a banker was not the objective. But—here's the second problem—*being novel* is an elusive and slippery concept. You can't hold onto novelty without it slipping away. For example, if you remain a banker for too long, then it's no longer novel. Then should we say you're no longer satisfying your objective? On the other hand, if your objective is to become a banker and you become a banker, then your objective is satisfied absolutely and it doesn't become any less clear the more time passes. Not only that, but if novelty was your "objective," you might have stepped through a number of professions on the road to becoming a banker, each one just as novel as the last with respect to what you had done in the past. Then you would be in the strange position of *already* having fulfilled your objective of novelty many times before you became a banker. In what sense then does becoming a banker matter towards fulfilling the "objective" of novelty? The problem is that viewing novelty as an objective requires awkward mental contortions even to come close to the usual way we think about objectives.

But there's really no need for such contortions. We're discussing the word "objective" here and words should be used to help us make important distinctions, not to cover them up or make them confusing. If you consider how novelty drives from simplicity to complexity, the whole process of searching for novelty is profoundly different from searching for a traditional objective. That's why we're forced into making such mental contortions in the first place when attempting to maintain "objective" as a blanket term for everything. Objectives are the traditional engines of achievement. Novelty is something different. So it makes sense to allow the words we use to help us to remember that distinction rather than to muddle it.

The same reasoning explains why "novelty" is a lot like "survive and reproduce" in natural evolution (which is also a kind of non-objective search): Both are constraints on what is possible that might be satisfied from the very beginning (just as single-celled organisms satisfied the "objective" of surviving and reproducing), both make discoveries that were never set as their initial objective, and both have no clear objective at all. Those are the telltale signs of non-objective search.

Another important and powerful property of these kinds of non-objective processes is their connection to the idea of *divergence* and divergent search. Objectives by their nature cause a search process to converge—towards the objective. And convergence means that many potentially interesting directions will not be explored. However, without the burden of the objective the search is free to branch in many directions and thereby diverge while collecting new stepping stones along the way. While divergence abandons the comfort of probing only in one predetermined direction, it is no coincidence that the term *divergent thinking* is associated with creativity and innovation. It is for the very reason that divergent thinkers do not become trapped in a stale corner of the search space that they are known for fearless and surprising discoveries that others tend to miss. By foregoing explicit final objectives, novelty search becomes a form of divergent search, thereby joining company with natural evolution and human innovation, and aligning it with this more exotic and radical form of discovery.

*   *   *

As we said earlier, from a scientific perspective a major appeal of the idea of novelty search is that it can actually be tested by implementing it as a computer algorithm, which is exactly what we did [49]. In fact, to date novelty search has been tested in a large number of different scenarios, but the first test was in a simulation of a robot in a maze. In other words, we programmed the computer to mimic the

Fig. 5.2 Robot Maze. The
large circle represents the
starting position of the robot
and the *small circle*
represents the goal.
Cul-de-sacs in the map that
appear to lead toward the goal
create deception.

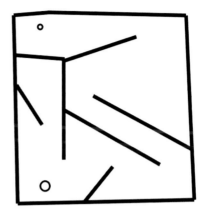

conditions of a robot in a walled maze, similarly to how driving simulators mimic the conditions of a car on a road. It's like a simple video game that the computer plays by itself. Experiments in simulation are common in the field of AI because the simulated robot can try new behaviors over and over again very rapidly and with no risk of damage. A diagram of one of the mazes is shown in Fig. 5.2.

So now imagine a wheeled robot trying novelty search in the maze, always trying to do something new. How does that actually work? The basic idea is that the computer program can generate new "ideas" for behaviors that the robot will try. If the behavior turns out to be novel when the robot tries it, then the behavior might be interesting so the program considers it a good idea. Note that this way of judging the quality of an idea is different from when there is a specific objective. For example, if the objective was for the robot to travel from the start position to the end of the maze, then "good" behavior would end up closer to the end of the maze than before.

The question of what behavior is good or not good is important because the good ideas are the ones that the program will explore further. In other words, the hope for novelty search is that good ideas could be stepping stones to something interesting. So after trying a bunch of behaviors, the program then decides to concentrate on the ones that seemed interesting. To do that, it takes those novel ideas and slightly alters them to see if something even more interesting and novel comes out. For example, if the robot goes around a wall it's never gone around before, then chances are that a slight modification of that behavior might go even further. On the other hand, if the robot does something it's done many times before, like crash into a wall, then that behavior is ignored and not explored further. This way of focusing on the more novel ideas for how to travel around a maze is similar to any other kind of creative thinking: You may have an interesting idea and then after thinking about it for a while realize that it opens up other interesting ideas.

Here's where the experiment becomes more intriguing: Imagine if the robot keeps trying new behaviors and explores the most novel behaviors even further. It's a lot like the robot we described earlier in the chapter that keeps crashing into walls until it figures out how to avoid crashing, and then learns to go through doorways. The question is, if we keep this kind of process going, would it eventually discover a behavior that solves a whole maze (in other words, a behavior that drives the robot all the way from start to finish) even though solving the maze is not its objective?

It turns out that the answer is yes—if we run novelty search for a while, the computer will consistently produce behaviors that drive the robot through the entire maze. That's an interesting result because no one programmed the robot to drive through the maze and also, more importantly, driving to the goal was never an objective. The program never even knew there was a goal. So it's interesting that novelty search ends up discovering a behavior that looks quite intelligent even though no one ever told the computer what the robot should do.

But the plot thickens even more from there because novelty search wasn't the only algorithm we attempted with the robot in the maze. We also tried a traditional objective-based approach in which the closer a behavior came to driving the robot to the goal, the better that behavior is considered. In other words, the behaviors that are explored further are the ones that push the robot closer to the goal. That's similar to how most objective-based activities work: You invest your time and energy in behaviors that bring you closer to your objective.

If you're a fan of objectives and believe they're important for achieving any serious accomplishment, you might reason that the objective-based approach would at least discover behaviors that travel to the goal more reliably than novelty search, which doesn't even have a goal. But that actually isn't how the experiment turned out. In fact, novelty search was much more reliable at finding behaviors that solve the maze. To be specific, we repeated the experiment with novelty search 40 times and in 39 of them a robot behavior was discovered that solves the maze. The result with objective-based search: three times out of 40.

It may seem surprising that attempting to find a behavior that solves the maze fails so often while *not trying* succeeds so consistently. Is there some flaw in the experimental setup? As you might expect, in the scientific community this kind of question has been debated many times since the initial maze experiments and much of the detail of such discussions can be found now in the scientific literature [49]. But the result turns out to have a solid basis that follows much of the logic of this book so far: Focusing only on the objective leads to deception. Robots that come closer to the goal are often actually running into cul-de-sacs that are far from the correct path to the real solution. These cul-de-sacs, which you can see in Fig. 5.2, are like any other deceptive trap—they're really no different from being stuck in a Chinese finger trap. The direction that *seems* to bring you closer ends up being the wrong direction. On the other hand, novelty search doesn't have this problem because it doesn't have any goal to deceive it. It just keeps finding behaviors that lead to new behaviors. Eventually one of them just happens to be the behavior of a robot that solves the maze.

Some people feel that the deception in the maze is too obvious, that it's set up somehow intentionally to be tricky. But really it's no more tricky than any other deceptive problem—which means just about any problem that's interesting. Still, to satisfy those who still needed convincing, we did try novelty search in a more natural scenario—a biped robot. In other words, we tried looking for novel behaviors for a two-legged simulated robot [49].

If your first question is, "What was the biped robot trying to do?" then you're forgetting that novelty search isn't trying to do anything in particular. It just looks at what the robot is doing and tries new versions of behaviors that were novel when they were discovered. So if the robot falls on its face, that's good as long as the robot never fell down before in the same way. What do you think a biped robot looking for novelty would eventually end up doing?

It turns out that the answer is that the robot learned to walk (Fig. 5.3). In fact, it learned to walk better than when it tried to learn with the objective of walking. In other words, a robot that tried to walk farther and farther actually ended up walking less far than one that simply tried to do something novel again and again. As usual the reason is because of deception: The stepping stones to walking aren't necessarily good walking, or even balancing. Falling down and kicking your legs may be a better stepping stone than trying to take a step (because kicking your legs is the foundation

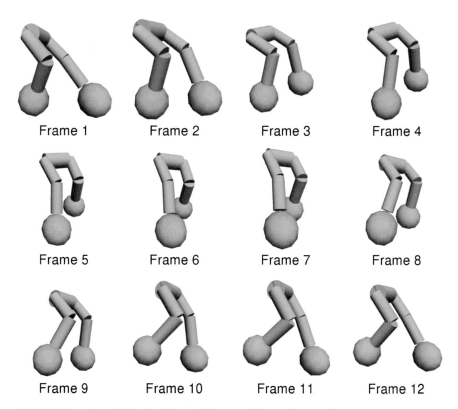

Fig. 5.3 One cycle of a biped walking gait discovered by novelty search.

of oscillation, which is how walking works), but if walking is the objective, falling down is considered one of the worst things you can do. So once again novelty search far outperformed the objective-based search.

Interestingly, the maze and biped results with novelty search didn't stand alone for long as researchers from around the world also began applying novelty search. Scientists in France led by Jean Baptiste Mouret replicated the results presented in the maze experiments [50]. In Canada, John Doucette applied novelty search to evolving computer programs that controlled artificial ants trying to follow a trail of food [51]. In the Czech Republic, Peter Krcah found that novelty search helped to solve deceptive problems when searching not only the behaviors but also designing the bodies of simulated robots [52]. In the United States, Heather Goldsby used novelty search to find bugs in computer programs [53]. And in our own lab in Florida, our colleague Sebastian Risi found that robots that learn during their lifetime and adapt to their circumstances can also benefit from novelty search [54]. From its wide applications, it has become clear that the results in the maze and biped experiments weren't flukes, but instead evidence that in general novelty search may sometimes yield a better result than searching for a specific objective. So it's often possible to achieve more by not trying to achieve it, and now we have experimental evidence to back it up.

Of course, there have also been demonstrations of the limitations of novelty search. It's no magic bullet and cannot solve every problem. In further experiments in the maze domain, we generated hundreds of random mazes of different difficulties and applied both novelty search and objective-based search to solving them. The trend that resulted from the data was that as mazes grow increasingly complicated, both novelty search and objective-based search can fail to solve them. However, objective-based search's abilities taper off much faster [55]. In other words, the reach of novelty search is greater but not unlimited. This result raises a deep question: What can be done then for the most complicated problems, what approach is left that can consistently solve them?

Maybe there isn't really a satisfying answer to this question. The idea that there's a single cure-all method for success that always gets you where you want to go is so enticing that it absorbs a huge amount of human passion and energy. It's like the empty quests of past explorers for the fountain of youth. But it just might be that we've been looking at the whole issue from the wrong perspective. Maybe you simply can't always get what you want when you want it. Perhaps there is no magic bullet that can always reach each and every objective that can be imagined. Ultimately, there may be futility at the heart of search, as the next chapter will explore. But even if there is no magic bullet, that doesn't stop us from finding things that are interesting anyway. Countless treasures are buried along the path to nowhere in particular. We can still dig them out and enjoy them even if we can't control what they are or when we find them. That's the real lesson of the interesting and the novel. But to see it most clearly, we need to appreciate the futility that lurks behind all methods of discovery, so that we can finally liberate ourselves from the fantasy of the elusive magic bullet and embrace the reality of the much more powerful *treasure hunter*.

Chapter 6
Long Live the Treasure Hunter

Je ne cherche pas, je trouve.

Pablo Picasso

Not everything is possible. You can't jump twelve feet in the air. And while many children dream of becoming an astronaut, only a few will actually pilot a spacecraft. Impossibility isn't a popular topic in our culture, where we say that you can be anything that you want to be, do anything if you put your mind to it. But in this chapter we'll stare impossibility straight in the eye—though we won't sacrifice our optimism in exchange. Instead, we'll discover a source of optimism that *embraces* the uncertainty of the far future rather than fearing or denying it. This journey begins by considering both the power and limitations of searching for novelty.

It might seem like the lesson of novelty search is that finding the objective is often easier when not looking for it. You might even solve more problems by not worrying about them instead of actually trying to solve them. So if you look at it that way, novelty search might seem to be just a new tool that can be added to the existing toolbox for achieving objectives. And it's true that some of the computer experiments with novelty search do actually produce this kind of outcome: The maze-navigating robot learns to solve mazes best when it's not trying to solve them; the biped learns to walk farthest when it's not trying to walk.

But we need to be careful how we interpret these results—what they seem to say on the surface is possibly misleading. We should be especially cautious when scientific results introduce something strange and new. Just as a car is not merely a new kind of horse, novelty search is not just a new or better way of reaching an objective. While the evidence clearly shows that *sometimes* you can do better without a specific objective, a deeper point is that of course novelty search will *not* always find what you want. Surely we can concoct problems where wandering without a care in the space of all possibilities fails to stumble upon a particular objective.

For example, imagine letting novelty search roam in an endless maze that stretches to the horizon in every direction. If you choose a particular place in this massive maze, what chance does novelty search have of discovering a behavior that goes to that *specific* place? (Experiments have indeed shown it can be lost in such

© Springer International Publishing Switzerland 2015
K.O. Stanley, J. Lehman, *Why Greatness Cannot Be Planned*,
DOI 10.1007/978-3-319-15524-1_6

cases [56].) This kind of possible failure illustrates that it's important not to expect too much: Novelty search is *not* a solution to all our problems—even though it might sometimes work better than pursuing a particular objective.

While this more realistic view of novelty search makes sense, the myth of the objective still shows its true colors when searching for an objective still performs *worse* than novelty search. Think about it this way: Pressing forward towards a far-off objective can't be a great idea when in many simple problems that approach fares *worse* than searching for nothing in particular. Still, it's hard to let go of the idea that objectives are useful. So you might be tempted to argue for a more charitable view of objectives. One possible argument is that objectives are still as necessary as ever, and that novelty search only highlights that there's a need to avoid putting all our eggs in one basket—that is, a need for a diversity of ideas while searching for something. In other words, because the single-minded pursuit of an objective is too deceptive, it's probably a good idea to keep many different alternatives around, just in case the paths that look the best at first don't work out.

One way to see this "moral of diversity" is to imagine betting on horses at a race track. Because even the best horses don't win every race, it might be better to play it safe by betting on a few horses (which gives you a diversity of possible paths to winning) rather than only on the one you most expect to win. If we think about novelty search in this way—just as a way to keep more options open—then we wouldn't have to give up on objectives entirely. Instead, all we'd need to do if we're actively pursuing an objective is keep around a variety of alternative stepping stones, just to be safe.

This view is kind to objectives. If you buy it, then you basically believe that although objectives may not be perfect, their guidance is still in general very useful. For example, objectives might be compared to a spelling rule such as '*i* before *e*, except after *c*': It's useful more often than not to heed its advice, even if in some rare cases it's misleading. So in this line of reasoning, it might be possible to patch up objective-based search instead of entirely abandoning it. In this spirit, one idea is that a *hybrid* of objective-driven search and novelty search might work well: The objective can help you stay on track while novelty search can prevent deception. Maybe then the lesson is that yes, we shouldn't rely on objective pressure alone, but we shouldn't abandon it entirely either.

Unfortunately it's not that simple. It would be nice if the world worked this way and we could simply keep our objectives by softening them with a little bit more diversity in the ideas we try out, but there's still a big problem: The more ambitious our objectives, the more deceptive they become as well. Deception is just a very nasty beast. And when you're dealing with deception, *by definition* the objective is a false compass. So no matter how much you do to convince yourself that you can keep your objective as long as you're still open-minded, that doesn't undo the fact that the objective is pointing in the wrong direction. If your compass points south but you're actually facing north, all the open-mindedness in the world won't change the fact that the compass is essentially useless. It's true that being open-minded might still get you where you need to go, for example if you sometimes ignore your compass and try a path here or there just to see where it goes. But the point is, if you do that and then end up actually reaching your destination, it was no thanks to your compass after all. You may as well have discarded it long ago.

Take for instance the robot searching for novel behaviors in the maze in the last chapter (Fig. 5.2). While it might be a stretch to call the objective of running through the maze ambitious, it turns out that it's still deeply deceptive anyway—when the robot tries to solve the maze as its objective, it almost always fails. Why is the objective even in a relatively simple maze so deceptive? The answer has to do with walls—when walls block the robot from running straight to the target, the objective-driven robot will crash into the closest wall in the direction of the goal.

This closest wall *attracts* the robot because by approaching it the robot edges closer to the goal—which is its objective—causing its reward to go up. But to come *any closer* to the goal than the wall allows would require first driving *much farther away*. But that won't work out well because moving away from the wall looks *worse* to the objective-driven search. So any further exploration of the idea of going around the wall is likely to be cut off prematurely. The problem is that the only time the objective actually pushes the search in the correct direction is at *the very end*, when the robot has learned to navigate to a point within a straight shot of the goal. But at that point the problem becomes trivial anyway: Learning to run towards a goal that is directly in front of you is not what one would call a challenge. Outside that small area where the goal is within a straight shot, the objective remains a false compass, whether or not it's combined with novelty search. So while it's true that combining the objective with a notion of novelty might work from time to time, it's definitely not a cure for the most ambitious problems. Such problems are so full of deception that the objective becomes a total liability, just as a fictional map offers no help even to the smartest explorer—they may still succeed, but no thanks to the map.

For example, you've heard us mention before the objective of attempting to build a computer five thousand years ago, which is just the kind of false map we're talking about: Back then, no amount of open-mindedness would lead to investing time in inventing vacuum tubes. Because who could have predicted that vacuum tubes would have anything at all to do with computation? It would make a lot more sense to invest in *all* interesting innovations, which is in fact just what humans did. So the idea that we simply need more diversity—but still should focus on objectives overall—is a false promise. The problem is that it denies an unavoidable inconvenience: A false compass remains false no matter how far you meander from its path.

That's why there's no easy way to interpret novelty search without letting go of some faith in objectives. While simply searching for novelty is definitely *not* a solution to every problem (even if it works some of the time), combining a drive for novelty with a drive towards the objective won't cure deception either. And of course objectives on their own are even worse. So we're going to have to accept something slightly humbling: Maybe the whole idea that there is some kind of "best practice" for finding your objective is misguided. There may simply be futility at the heart of search—*no* approach to searching can guarantee that you reach your objectives. It's not enough to give up the idea that objectives are the *best* way to direct a search. We've seen that they're not. But we'll also have to abandon the idea that *anything* can always reveal the path to an ambitious objective.

While it's true that novelty search does a better job of finding robot behaviors that solve the maze or the biped walking problem, that doesn't mean that novelty search will always work. The more troubling lesson is that objective-driven search is sometimes embarrassingly incompetent. If setting an objective and then aiming for it is really the right path to achievement, then what does it say that an approach that doesn't even know what it's trying to do actually performs better in some simple problems? While you could point out that in much more difficult problems novelty search might also not perform well, the fact that objective-driven search is *already* failing in these simple problems means that its prospects are even bleaker. If it already falls behind in a simple maze-navigation domain then what hope does it have of discovering, for example, higher intelligence? Forget about evolving human intelligence from a single-celled organism—we can't even reliably train a simple robot to navigate a few hallways.

If you still want to defend objectives, there's another possible angle. You could argue that the computer program behind the objective-driven experiments might be flawed in some other way. Maybe there's a bug somewhere in the program that skews the results. But the experiments in the last chapter can't be dismissed so easily because other than the difference between seeking the objective and seeking only novelty, the programs were *exactly the same*. And because we know that the system *does* solve the mazes consistently when seeking novelty, the problem here can't be with another aspect of the program. We're looking at a situation in which an identical algorithm searches in both cases and succeeds only when looking for novelty. What's more, the results have been verified by other researchers [50]. The only conclusion left is that the problem must be with the objective itself. And because novelty search isn't a solution for every problem, and a hybrid of novelty and the objective can also be only imperfect at best, we're left with the stark reality that *nothing* can reliably reach particular target objectives.

That may sound like bad news, but it isn't necessarily all that surprising—taken to the extreme, what kind of search could consistently find the one minuscule needle hidden somewhere within a skyscraper-sized haystack? In fact, much has been written on the limitations of search. For example, a famous principle called the *No Free Lunch Theorem* by David Wolpert and William Macready showed that there is no overall best algorithm for searching, not over all possible optimization problems [57]. In fact, it turns out that improving a search process to reach certain objectives will always hurt its performance on a different set of problems. In short, you really *can't* win them all.

For example, rules of thumb that usually help us make good decisions sometimes end up misleading us in certain special circumstances. Our car keys are not *always* where we last left them—not when the dog drags them off the table. Researchers in the field of machine learning, especially those interested in what's called "black box optimization," are familiar with these kinds of arguments.

But here's where novelty search takes the plot on a surprising twist. The situation may sound hopeless, but the conclusion is both more subtle and more profound than it seems: We *can* reliably find something amazing. We just *can't* say what that something is!

The insight is that great discoveries are possible if they're left undefined. This statement draws on the results from Picbreeder and from the processes of natural evolution and human innovation. It's true that the outcome for novelty search versus objective-driven search in the previous chapter casts a shadow over objectives. Those results showed that objectives can be outperformed by a more clever kind of objective ignorance. But the more important lesson of non-objective search is that it's a powerful *treasure hunter*. However, instead of finding a *particular* treasure that you might have in mind, as it diverges through the search space it finds *many* treasures, all of which may be surprises. The novelty search experiments confirm that some treasures that are difficult to reach through objectives can be more easily reached without them. But there's just no way to say exactly which treasures can be reached. All we know is that some places are within reach that otherwise would not be, whether they are places we want to visit or not. No one set out to discover the Picbreeder *Car*, but it was still discovered. To highlight the irony here, the *Car* never would have been discovered if someone *had* set out to find it.

This strange paradox, where trying is a curse and not trying is a blessing, sets the stage for a more realistic understanding of what is achievable and how. It means that ambitious goals can't reliably be achieved by trying—unless they are one stepping stone away, where they come within reach. Otherwise, the only choice that remains is *not* trying. And while this treasure-hunting approach will not ensure reaching any particular objective, what it *will* do is accumulate stepping stones that lead to unfamiliar places. The treasure hunter is an opportunistic explorer—searching for anything and everything of value, without a care for what might be found. To be a treasure hunter, you have to collect as many stepping stones as you can, because you never know which one might lead somewhere valuable.

And even if your own personal journey doesn't end where you had hoped, the idea of the solitary inventor striving relentlessly towards her inevitable objective was always a myth. Rather, it's the combination of many minds with many different interests that ultimately plunders the search space in the long run, not any individual objective or person. We can be confident that the *Butterflies* and *Cars* of our future will be found not because someone is looking for them, but because everyone is looking for everything. The future will arrive off schedule, but it will arrive nonetheless.

This insight may seem sad, that we're left with no sure compass, that all our efforts to create certainty and to search with purpose may be futile. But our disappointment may be misplaced. Perhaps search isn't really about objectives but about something much bigger. In that case, abandoning the false compass can be liberating, opening up a new frontier. Novelty search shows that it's possible to capture the process of open-ended innovation and divergent thinking even within a computer. So it can't be a mystical form of voodoo but rather a principled and logical process that we can understand and even capture. If discovery without explicit objectives is the guiding light of natural evolution, of human innovation, of Picbreeder and novelty search, then we might harness it for our own purposes. Instead of something to fear it can be something to embrace.

One implication of Picbreeder and novelty search is that we can actually build systems based on the non-objective principle. That's not something we've done very often in the past, but once we escape the myth of the objective, the possibility of building *treasure-hunting systems* becomes intriguing. They might help us discover useful or interesting possibilities that would otherwise lie hidden. Human feedback can even play a role, as it does in Picbreeder, capitalizing on our diverse tastes and insights. And once humans begin to contribute, a lot of practical possibilities open up.

The best way to harness the power of a group of people in the non-objective world isn't through brainstorming sessions or meetings or big ambitious projects. It's not about sitting down and coming to a *consensus* on what to do. That's not the treasure hunter—consensus is exactly the cultural tendency that we need to escape. We don't want "Top 40" lists where everyone tries to agree what the best songs are, nor "design by committee" where any interesting vision for a new product is watered down by consensus. No, the way to unleash the treasure hunter is actually through *separating* people from each other, like in Picbreeder, where people only interact by taking off from where someone else left. While many participants in such a treasure-hunting system might arrive with their own *personal* objectives, the *system* as a whole ends up lacking a unified objective because people's objectives differ.

For example, in Picbreeder it isn't bad that the images that one person breeds might be disliked by somebody else, because both people might separately contribute valuable stepping stones to the overall treasure hunt for interesting images. The idea is to collect stepping stones found through the diversity of preferences of everyone who participates. Interestingly, the internet provides an exciting opportunity to experiment with this kind of treasure hunting. With instantaneous global communication it becomes easier than ever to organize people all over the world to build off each other's creations.

For example, consider a website that sells furniture. If you visit this kind of site today, what you get is essentially an online catalog. You visit, browse through the offerings, and choose the item you want. In other words, the creative exchange is one-sided—you as the consumer purchase what someone else designs and markets to you. But someday things might work differently. At first it might seem like business as usual: If you were buying a chair then a set of available models would greet you. But after that, it would get more interesting—instead of choosing one model to buy as normal, you could request a set of *variations* of your favorite option. And these variations would not be mere customizations, like a choice of color or an inscribed saying, but a true *mutation* of an existing design that can vary in deep ways. For example, a new chair might have a new colorful pattern in its fabric or a new table might have legs that all bend in different ways.

These new variants would then be presented to you almost like a whole new catalog, but one generated based on the model *you* chose just before. Until you find something you want to buy, you could keep selecting favorites and viewing variants of them. The chair you finally request to purchase would end up truly shaped by your own creativity—your own choices helped to design it. It could then be custom-manufactured and shipped to your home. Unlike today's online catalogs, in this new world you're part of the creative process that previously excluded you. What's exciting is that you wouldn't have to be a talented woodworker or a professional designer anymore—you could personally *breed* a chair just as Picbreeder users breed pictures.

So far, the story only covers one customer. But with many customers coming to the site and ultimately buying chairs after breeding them, the magic of the treasure hunter begins to come out: The site becomes a stepping stone collection, a stockpile of discoveries in a growing database of chair designs, each one possibly a stepping stone to even more appealing chairs. And we *know* which chairs are the treasures because we know which chairs the customers ultimately buy. So when a new customer arrives, the initial presentation of available models can be a *collection of discoveries* bred and then purchased by previous customers. In this way, even if they don't realize it, the customers end up exploring the space of chairs together, jumping off from the favored discoveries of their predecessors. The old-fashioned online furniture catalog just became fresh and renewed: It's now a collaborative search with no unified objective—a treasure hunter.

Of course, this kind of treasure-hunting catalog can be applied to a lot more than just chairs. Clothing catalogs, automobile catalogs, and even custom housing could be explored this way. Even if such personally-tailored products might cost more to build, that's not the important point here. Manufacturing processes may have to catch up (perhaps aided by the rapid progress and increasing interest in three-dimensional printing machines), but when they do the point is that people will no longer be *restricted* to the designs of expert designers. Instead, they can discover their own novel designs, yielding genuinely unique articles unlike anything seen before.

But the reason we're talking about this kind of interactive catalog is not because it's a good business idea. More importantly, this thought experiment raises an intriguing question: Would you *trust* this kind of catalog? Would you trust a catalog in which essentially nothing is designed by an expert and everything is "discovered" by its users? What would you expect the collection of articles to be like? Could they possibly be worth your money or attention, or would they look like the second-rate dabbling of aimless amateurs?

Let's first get one detail out of the way: It's clear that someone would have to design the online system itself that allows the space of furniture (or whatever product space) to be explored. An artificial system of DNA would have to be programmed in some way to allow slight random variations of current candidate models to be generated. Only then would there be a meaningful space of furniture or chairs for users to explore. The idea would be similar to how Picbreeder creates slight random variations of images to allow users to explore new image possibilities. In the same way, the furniture site would need a way to represent furniture that can slightly mutate furniture designs—a set of digital furniture genes. We can't take for granted that writing a computer program to mutate furniture designs is very easy to begin with. It might very well take some trial and error to get it right, but the larger question is whether we would expect its users ever to discover desirable designs. Even if we assume that the space of furniture has been programmed well, and allows easy exploration of furniture space, there are still some potential problems. The explorers are still *not* furniture designers and also have no unified design goal among each other. So the question remains: What do we expect to come of such an experiment?

Naturally, this sounds risky for a furniture company—or any other business. Should a business really leave it to its customers to determine what products are designed and sold? But the evidence for the treasure hunter suggests that this type of system is exactly the right way to uncover the needles in the haystack. The lack of a unified objective means that the system won't be deceived by the appearance of improvement. It won't converge to only a few pieces of conventional furniture designed by the consensus of its users. Instead, it will accumulate stepping stones that lead to further stepping stones. Designers themselves, even professionals, can still be deceived when optimizing for a particular style or specification—the problem (as usual) is that the stepping stones to great design may not resemble the idealized final product. That's why even the experts probably will never contemplate many appealing kinds of designs. The irony is that inexperienced amateurs coming into the catalog with no unified objective whatsoever are for these reasons sometimes more likely to find the hidden treasures.

But that's not to say that professional designers will lose their jobs. Clearly their role is important and many of their designs are excellent and appropriate. But the point is that there are still possibilities out there that we will never discover through traditional means. *Those* hidden treasures are the ones that would be uncovered by the customers in the non-unified system. Systems like the evolving furniture catalog (that lack a unified overall purpose) are interesting because their participants don't follow our usual urge to unify and seek consensus in groups working towards specific goals. Instead the users are unleashed to diverge and build off each others' creations. And rather than removing the need for experts, perhaps someday their skills will be enlisted to help *create* and *extend* these kinds of systems in the first place. That way, their expertise can inform the construction of the space that customers will search.

The main point is that the treasure hunter can be harnessed to create and discover innovative concepts that otherwise would never exist. The interactive catalog is just one possible application (Chaps. 7 and 8 will hint at other applications of the idea). More importantly, the interactive catalog demonstrates that this way of thinking can yield new approaches to innovation that aren't based on traditional design principles. Yes, we must ultimately relinquish the idea that there exists some method that can guarantee our arrival at a predetermined destination. There's no magic formula for achievement, and that's the futility at the heart of search. But—the silver lining is that we can still find hidden treasure in distant lands by departing without a destination in mind. So we shouldn't mourn too deeply for the myth of the objective.

Search is at its most awesome when it has no unified objective. Just look at natural evolution, at human innovation, at Picbreeder, or at novelty search. These are not all the same process, and some are more grandiose than others, but they do share the single unifying theme that they have no objective. Novelty search in particular highlights the risk of overconfidence in objectives. And as we begin to liberate ourselves from their grip, many things will change about the way we see the world. The next two chapters explore the implications of this new way of thinking for how we run our society. Under the new light of innovation without objectives, many once-familiar principles will never be the same.

Chapter 7
Unshackling Education

You show me anything that depicts institutional progress in America: school test scores, crime stats, arrest reports, anything that a politician can run on, anything that someone can get a promotion on. And as soon as you invent that statistical category, fifty people in that institution will be at work trying to figure out a way to make it look as if progress is occurring when actually none is.

David Simon

As this book began we pointed out how almost everything in our culture is guided by objectives. They're so universal in our lives and our jobs that we hardly see the need to question them. But they're always affecting us, driving and coloring almost everything we do. And now we've seen how objectives can so easily deceive us. In the preceding chapters we've explored how Picbreeder and novelty search hint that discovery works best when free from the chains of objectives. Still, the big question remaining—to be explored over the next two chapters—is how objectives are impacting our lives today. On the surface, they may appear to grease the wheels of progress. But deeper down their cost is steep.

First in this chapter we'll make the general case for how the growing obsession with objectives can harm society. We all share some intuition that the constant polls, assessment, and reliance on objective measures tends to dehumanize and mechanize what once was creative. Of course, these side effects might grudgingly be accepted as the price of progress if they brought better outcomes. But we'll see that often results are *worse* when measures of society are set as explicit benchmarks. So without the boon of better results, there's little to be gained from doggedly chasing after flawed measures, and potentially much to lose.

Next, to make these hidden costs for society more concrete, the bulk of this chapter will examine in more detail a critical function of society: educating our children. We'll see how objective obsession can explain current unsettling trends in education, like the single-minded focus on standardized tests and the stripping of teacher autonomy. But of course current trends can also be reversed: We'll also see how non-objective thinking can bring a fresh perspective on education that embraces exploration, human diversity, and creativity.

© Springer International Publishing Switzerland 2015
K.O. Stanley, J. Lehman, *Why Greatness Cannot Be Planned*,
DOI 10.1007/978-3-319-15524-1_7

To begin, are there clear cases where defining overarching objectives for society do more harm than good? In fact, there's ample scientific evidence suggesting that this often occurs. For example, the quote beginning this chapter echoes Campbell's law, which is well known in the social sciences [58]: "The more any quantitative social indicator is used for social decision-making, the more subject it will be to corruption pressures and the more apt it will be to distort and corrupt the social processes it is intended to monitor."

In other words, social indicators like academic achievement tests are *least* effective exactly when the objective is to bring them *higher*. The problem is that a simple metric rarely captures the essence of what you really care about. For example, judging teachers from student performance on achievement tests encourages teaching directly to the test [59]. And the end result isn't students with meaningful knowledge and skills, but ones who are good at memorization and test-taking [60]. So while scores on the test might even *increase*, they can *mean less* at the same time [61]. Of course, there's much more to say about education, and we'll return to the topic in greater depth later in this chapter.

But *any* ambitious societal effort will end up confronting the same frustrating paradox. When the quest for progress is packaged into a measure, the result is an objective-driven approach. If the objective is ambitious, then a drive to increase objective performance is likely to produce deception, preventing the best possible result from being discovered. For example, GDP (gross domestic product) is a measure of national productivity. Of course, as a nation, the hope is to maximize GDP, which makes maximal GDP a kind of national objective. But once again, an increase in GDP does not mean that economic policies, if continued, will lead to even higher GDP. The economy could be stuck in a Chinese finger trap—a decrease might be needed to produce a much larger increase. In fact, economists recognize that relying too heavily upon GDP makes little sense—even while in practice it is the most widely-touted economic indicator. This paradox has been called "GDP fetishism [62]."

Like test scores, indicators like GDP can become less meaningful as they are directly optimized. The problem is that because GDP is such a simple measure, it doesn't truly capture what really makes for a healthy economy. A sneaky politician seeking re-election might institute policies sure to significantly boost GDP in the short term but that are poisonous to the economy in the long term. These kind of problems just go to show the danger in guiding national policy through simple measures—they can easily result in deception.

A more poisonous and extreme form of Campbell's law is the problem of *perverse incentives*. Strangely, sometimes rewards or measures chosen to make things better actually make them far worse. For example, when India was under British rule, the British government tried to exterminate poisonous snakes by paying citizens for every dead snake they handed over. But it didn't work out the way it was intended: Instead it led to citizens literally breeding cobras just to kill them for the bounty. Ultimately, the number of venomous snakes in India actually *increased* [63].

So the incentive system produced the opposite of the intended effect. And the same thing happened in Hanoi but with rats—leading not to fewer rats, but to *rat farms* [64].

There are plenty of other examples of perverse incentives: Campaigns aiming to reduce abusing alcohol or drugs can result in the abuse of more dangerous drugs instead [65]; paying workers for each fragment of dinosaur bone they find leads to smashing whole bones [66]; and paying executives with bonuses for higher earnings leads to short-term profits but long-term disaster [67]. These examples show that deception isn't confined to algorithms and evolution, but is widespread. It's very much a danger for everyday society. The question is how deeply the myth of the objective hurts our society, and what we can do about it.

As we begin to discuss human society, of course we should proceed with special care. It's not every day that an insight first uncovered in an online picture-breeding website ends up informing cultural behavior. Congress doesn't traditionally legislate based on the latest breakthroughs in mathematical theory. Abstract science and social critique rarely meet, at least outside a Google search. But somehow their intersection here is surprisingly natural. Maybe it's because the quest for achievement is at heart so human, even while scientists study achievement and discovery too.

What we've been examining all along throughout this book is the logic of discovery. And of course the pursuit of any worthy goal must follow some kind of inner logic. In some cases the logic is so weak that it's already widely discredited, like how obsession with standardized tests in education can result in improvements mainly in test-taking skills and memorization [59–61]. In other cases it's more subtle and less discussed. The greatest danger is when the logic is wrapped within a lofty objective, lending it instant credibility and seemingly putting it beyond question. It might seem pointlessly radical to question cultural staples like measuring progress or assessing plans for how likely they are to succeed. Who could be against assessment?

But we've seen that something is wrong with objectives and that the problem is not suddenly going to go away because they're wrapped up in the best of human intentions. It's also worrying that non-objective discovery is so often effective when objective-driven striving isn't. So we've come to a point where we have the special (and exciting) privilege of questioning the unquestionable. While there's no doubt that this kind of contrary thinking can be fun, at the same time we'll try not to lose our humility. We're not aiming to condemn the entire foundation of modern society. As we've noted before, objectives are not and will never be useless. They play an important role in day-to-day modest achievement and will continue to do so. But we're not talking about that kind of achievement here.

Instead, we're examining those pockets where people are striving for innovation, discovery, and creativity. In other words, we're interested in the distant shore on the far side of the mist-cloaked lake. And because creativity is so central to what makes us human, we can find these kinds of efforts almost everywhere, from the halls of elementary schools or research universities to the portfolios of investors—and even within ourselves. But while we can find creativity and innovation almost everywhere, it's helpful to explore particular instances to show how non-objective thinking can bring specific insights that could directly impact society. In particular, the next chapter will focus on human innovation through science, business, and art, while the remainder of this chapter will examine education.

*   *   *

As a step towards questioning how education is treated by society, let's begin by looking at the stereotype of the aimless youth. You probably know the type—or perhaps even you were the type: no clear path to the future, no concrete goals. These are the kids we're not supposed to imitate. To get your act together you need to have a plan and a purpose, and then you're supposed to pursue it whole-heartedly. But aren't distant career aspirations themselves ambitious objectives? The steps from teenage honor roll to great inventor are anything but certain. If you begin life striving for a fancy future career and let this quest guide all your choices, chances are that you'll sooner or later collide with deception (as with any ambitious objective search). Sure, you might end up with a Masters degree in engineering and a job at a respectable company—but if that's all you accomplish then you're not the great inventor you started out dreaming to become.

And at this point in the book we have some idea why that is. It's not simply that the goal is difficult and that you didn't try hard enough. Instead it's the more sinister problem of deception—the steps that *lead* to great invention aren't likely to *resemble* great invention. You were navigating by the false compass. At the same time, we've seen that often a search without objectives leads to more interesting results. Strangely, perhaps you might have come closer to the realm of great inventor (or great architect, or great composer) if only you had imitated the aimless youth after all. The aimless youth can play the treasure hunter, liberated to survey the stepping stones and choose the most interesting. Anyone whose path isn't fixed from the start can explore stepping stones and pursue those that they find most interesting in the moment. The aimless have the opportunity to smell the roses and consume knowledge broadly. That opportunity was lost on the overachiever focused only on marking the next box on the checklist of life.

A lot of common assumptions, like the supposed danger of aimlessness, start looking more uncertain if you accept that the objective compass is a myth. Of course, the story is never simple—being aimless isn't *always* a good idea, but when it's paired with a thirst for exploration, it might indeed hint at great potential. And now, after seeing so many examples of great discoveries without explicit objectives, we have some idea why that is. With this perspective, success stories like that of Steve Jobs make perfect sense—in his own words:

> After six months, I couldn't see the value in it. I had no idea what I wanted to do with my life and no idea how college was going to help me figure it out. And here I was spending all of the money my parents had saved their entire life. So I decided to drop out and trust that it would all work out okay. It was pretty scary at the time, but looking back it was one of the best decisions I ever made. The minute I dropped out I could stop taking the required classes that didn't interest me, and begin dropping in on the ones that looked interesting.

Does this mean everyone should drop out of college? No, but it does mean that not having a plan can be a very good plan. If you're out to explore the interesting, hunting down the most promising stepping stones, your strategy is as valid as taking the pre-med route with all the required classes. Even though Steve Jobs said that he had no idea what he wanted to do, he did *exactly* what he wanted to do, which was to explore. It's just that in our culture "exploring" without a clear objective seems so flawed and misguided that not even Steve Jobs had the words to say it positively. Who knows what the next generation might discover without the weight of all the usual milestones and plans upon them?

Stories of free-thinking trailblazers like Steve Jobs show it's possible to buck the traditional path to higher education and still be successful. But more importantly, this kind of story illustrates the deep shadow that objective thinking casts over education in general. In this sense, education happens to make an easy target because its heavy reliance on *assessment* is really all about pursuing objectives. There are so many types of assessment in the education system as a whole that it would be mundane to pick on some of the most obvious. For example, we all know that constant childhood testing might stifle creativity. But instead of choosing such easy targets, let's look more deeply at how the myth of the objective lurks behind even widely accepted practices. In particular, instead of considering the effect of student testing on *students*, let's think for a moment about how and why *schools* themselves are assessed based on the results of standardized test scores.

Assessment is currently the rage in education. Standardized tests are used not only to assess students, but to assess the success of the schools in educating them. Often the hope is that such school assessment will help lead to desirable *outcomes*, which are essentially educational objectives. For example, a 2008 letter to the Commissioner of the Florida Department of Education from the United States Department of Education discusses progress in the state of Florida towards the objectives of No Child Left Behind:

> Annual measurable objectives (AMO) (the yearly target for the percentage of students required to be proficient or above for a school to make AYP [adequate yearly progress]):
>
> - 2008–09: Florida's goal for this year is 65 percent of students scoring proficient in reading/language arts and 68 percent in mathematics.
> - AMO type: Florida set its AMOs consistent with the statutory requirements, using an annual adjustment. This means that AMOs increase in equal increments every year [68].

Notice the emphasis on specific, measurable objectives. One way to think about this approach is that the state is basically setting its own educational stepping stones. One year the stepping stone is 65 % and 68 % proficiency. The next year it may be higher. The hope is that the numbers will climb steadily upward towards the long-term objective: nearly *every* student being proficient. The assumption is that *increasing performance* indicates progress towards the ambitious goal of *near-perfect performance* in the future. But notice that's the same kind of assumption that leads to fingers stuck within a Chinese finger trap—the assumption that the path to freedom *can never* pass through something appearing less free. It's the same flawed reasoning behind objective-based search in general, that improving objective performance lights the path to the objective.

But when we're talking about important pillars of society like education, it can be difficult to swallow the flaws in objective thinking. If improving objective performance isn't the path to achievement, then what can we possibly do to hold ourselves "accountable?" We want simple objective measures to tell us if a teacher or a school is doing a good job, so we can reward improving performance and punish performance that declines. But unfortunately, the more complicated the problem is, the less likely it is that the myth of the objective will hold true—and education is definitely a very complicated social problem. So while no serious educator believes that education is a simple problem, driving progress by objectives would only make sense if the problem *was* simple.

There's no reason to believe that the ambitious objectives of education are somehow immune to deception. While it sounds strange, if a particular class scores *higher* on a given test than last year, it might be no better than if they'd scored *lower* instead—when considering the brightness of the school's long-term future. The problem is that the stepping stones to genuinely *fantastic* classroom-wide performance are likely completely unrelated to any common educational metric: Tests try to force everyone to better resemble the desired fantastic *outcome* (i.e. objective), which we've seen is often a formula for getting stuck. In other words, measuring performance against any ambitious objective leads to deception, so the underpinnings of the whole enterprise depend upon the myth of the objective. That's one reason why it's so important to recognize deception's undercurrents in objective-driven achievement—they impact even broad social efforts, and the damage done might not be otherwise recognized for a long time.

For example, a similar drive towards measurement hit the field of software engineering (the business of making new software) when it was young. In the field's early days, many focused on the promise of concrete measurements to increase productivity and software quality. An influential book written in 1982 by Tom DeMarco exemplifies this movement, which can be characterized by its most famous quote: "You can't control what you can't measure [69]." Over 35 years later, DeMarco published an article revealing that his viewpoint had reversed over time: While "the book's deep message seems to be, metrics are good, more would be better, and most would be best," it turns out that they "must be used with careful moderation [70]." With more complex software, composed of millions of lines of code and countless interacting parts, simple metrics become uninformative. In the same article, DeMarco writes that although metrics allow for control, strict control is only important or appropriate when working on a project with little chance of major impact [70]—in other words, measurements are great when you have a modest goal, but lose their value when applied naively to ambitious undertakings. The result of all the metric obsession in software was that engineers were required to wrestle measures upwards, even as they understood that the metrics were becoming increasingly disconnected from reality—and it took many frustrating years for that objective tide to begin to ebb. It's possible that the same lesson in simplified objective measures is currently being played out in the United States educational system, but with children and teachers chained to deceptive measures of achievement instead of engineers.

But the problem isn't just that deception can undermine major efforts like education. There are also other more subtle injuries from objective-based thinking in social efforts. For example, another pillar of the recent push for accountability is that assessment and its aims can be improved by making it more *accurate*. Take for instance the Obama administration's Race to the Top educational initiative, which the Department of Education touts for its emphasis on accuracy:

> Authorized under the ARRA, the Race to the Top Assessment program provides funding to consortia of States to develop assessments that are valid, support and inform instruction, provide accurate information about what students know and can do, and measure student achievement against standards designed to ensure that all students gain the knowledge and skills needed to succeed in college and the workplace [71].

Higher education is also moving towards the same kind of assessment-driven culture with new tests like the Collegiate Learning Assessment (CLA) and the Collegiate Assessment of Academic Proficiency (CAAP) [72, 73]. These tests also aim to provide an accurate picture of progress and achievement, now at the college level.

But there's a problem with accuracy that's also tied to the myth of the objective: Surprisingly, accuracy doesn't necessarily help increase performance in a pursuit driven by objectives. That's probably not the kind of news you want to hear if you're involved in the push for more accuracy in assessment. But the bright side is that if accuracy doesn't cure the problem with ambitious objectives then at least we can redirect resources to something more promising.

You may recall the *Skull* image that was bred by users of Picbreeder in Chap. 3. It's an interesting example because it will help us see why accuracy can't be the cure. What's of particular interest are the stepping stones that actually led to the *Skull* when it was bred in Picbreeder (shown in Fig. 7.1). The important observation is that most of them look *nothing* like a skull. One is a crescent shape, another looks like a donut, and another resembles a dish. So to get to the *Skull*, the users first had to discover these seemingly unrelated images.

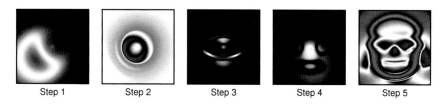

Step 1   Step 2   Step 3   Step 4   Step 5

Fig. 7.1 Images that eventually led to the *Skull* image. These steps (sampled from the total set of 74 steps) trace the origin of the Picbreeder *Skull* back to its primordial roots

Now imagine that we launched a nationwide effort to breed the *Skull* again from scratch. The US Department of Skull Breeding sets rigorous standards for encouraging progress, mandating the most accurate assessment possible for every image bred. To satisfy this requirement, a panel of world-class researchers in *Skull* rating develop a cutting-edge test to measure the *Skull*-ness of any candidate image on a scale from 0 to 100. With the security of this highly accurate test the nation can now breed boldly towards a new era of *Skull*-like images. Newly bred images that score poorly should confidently be thrown away while those with higher scores should clearly be bred further.

Unfortunately, we already know where this effort will lead. If we're lucky, it may lead to some interesting places, but where it won't lead is the *Skull*. You can see exactly why it can never work by looking at the stepping stones in Fig. 7.1—they don't look like skulls! So it doesn't matter how accurately we can assess the *Skull*-ness of an image because the stepping stones to a good *Skull* don't look anything like the *Skull* anyway. (In fact, this prediction was confirmed in experiments that tried exactly the idea of rewarding *Skull*-like images, which led to consistent failure [37].) The problem in particular here is that the thing we're comparing against (a skull) looks nothing like the steps that lead to it (a crescent, a donut, and a dish). So accuracy does *nothing* for us when we have such a fundamentally broken compass. The result is just a better estimate of what remains a distraction.

Beyond only the *Skull* in Picbreeder, as we've seen repeatedly in past chapters, it's a general property of search that the stepping stones to a great achievement don't resemble that final thing: Vacuum tubes don't resemble computers and flatworms don't resemble humans. As usual, all these examples boil down the same story of deception in complex search spaces.

Tying the argument back to education, there's little doubt that the problem of achieving a nation of exceptionally well-educated students is much more complex than the problem of breeding the *Skull*. For the very same reasons, educational assessment is also unlikely to benefit from increasing accuracy: The assessment merely measures *how well current performance compares to ideal performance*. Just as with the *Skull*, or the robot in the maze in Chap. 5, regardless of accuracy, the result is likely a quick convergence to a mediocre dead end. Contrary to intuitions, we can conclude that assessment accuracy is *unimportant* in these kinds of problems. While it sounds strange, it starts to make sense if you realize that *objectivity* itself is sometimes counterproductive. In such cases, of course accuracy no longer serves a useful master.

*   *   *

In addition to misguided confidence in *accurate* measurement, another subtle injury resulting from objective-based thinking in education is the drive towards *uniform standards*. The intuitive idea is that every student should have access to the same type and quality of education no matter where they live. The driving force is equality: A student living in the Northeast should receive an equivalent education as one living in the West or South. In other words, schools everywhere should have the same set of standards for what they teach their students. That way, no matter where they live, all students can learn the same concepts and can be equally prepared for work or higher education when they graduate from high school.

Applying the same idea a different way motivates *uniform assessments* of student performance conducted regularly. That way, there is a common benchmark even across the entire geography of a country, and many concrete measurements to map the progress of individual students and their teachers across their careers. So if students in one area are getting a worse education, or teachers in a particular school are not performing well, the problem will become clearly visible. The idea is that uniform assessments can assist achieving equality, and at the same time enable clearer comparisons and increased rigor.

An example of the drive towards uniform standards is the "Common Core State Standards Initiative," sponsored by the National Governors Association (among others) and developed in partnership with Achieve, Inc. The main goal of Common Core is to establish a uniform set of national standards for teaching, and a corresponding set of regular and uniform assessments [74]. Although controversial, Common Core has already been adopted by a great majority of US states, reflecting the intuitive appeal of increased accountability, quantification, and uniformity. And while on the surface such uniformity may appear beneficial, beneath the surface lies the familiar myth of the objective.

In fact, an explicit purpose of Common Core's educational standards is to establish objectives, as reflected in the FAQ from the Common Core website: "Educational standards help teachers ensure their students have the skills and knowledge they need to be successful by providing clear goals for student learning [74]." And of course, what use are objectives unless progress towards them can be often and accurately measured, and made uniform for easy and universal comparison? For this reason, Common Core aids the "the development and implementation of common comprehensive assessment systems to measure student performance annually that will replace existing state testing systems [74]."

While it is easy to appreciate the good intentions behind the drive for uniform standards, at this point it may also be easy to see how good intent is undermined by the myth of the objective. Uniformity is much like accuracy. It's a warm companion of assessment and measurement, but a strong adversary of the treasure hunter.

A truly uniform educational system would make every student's experience more equal in a trivial sense: Their lessons, goals, and tests would be the same. However, blanket uniformity, while perhaps lending the secure feeling of increased objectivity and scientific rigor, has no necessary connection to improving your child's education. Whatever standard is chosen to be made uniform could be good, or it could be bad. Of course, instituting a bad standard would make the overall situation worse, but let's assume the best: Even if the standard is well-chosen and reflects current best practices, those current best practices will likely be rooted in the mythology of objectives.

Think of it this way: Whatever sequence of standardized tests the Common Core initiative converges upon, will the simple resulting statistics point the way to world-class education? If we believe that measuring and encouraging progress through standardized tests is a broken compass in general, why focus on applying one particular version of that broken compass more uniformly? The only effect is that students everywhere will come to be graded by exactly the same misleading measurements (that do not lead to the ultimate objective even when accurate), and education everywhere will aim towards achieving the same deceptive objectives. So unless we're sure we have uncovered an ultimate solution to the overwhelmingly complex problem of education, the yardsticks and objectives we converge to will be yet another broken compass, only this time it will be rebranded with the shiny official stamp of "gold standard." It's just another version of the same flawed reasoning that would seek more *accurate* broken compasses. The lesson is that a misleading measurement tool doesn't improve when it's made more accurate or adopted universally.

However, imposing uniformity also inflicts more subtle wounds, because beyond having no inherent benefits, it also undermines making *future* discoveries. Enforcing uniform standards means *converging* to a single standard. It means extinguishing the diversity of alternative standards that individual schools or states might currently be exploring. As a result, it becomes more likely that future standards and tests will be limited to tweaks of the imposed status quo—because it is the only one applied and explored by teachers in their classrooms.

We can relate this lack of diversity in exploration to the novelty search algorithm described in Chap. 5. When a single measure of progress is uniformly applied to a search for robots able to navigate through the maze in Fig. 5.2, the result is quick convergence to a deceptive dead-end. But when novelty is encouraged and many divergent possibilities for success are simultaneously explored, the result is consistent discovery of a solution. Of course, in education we might not want any crazy novelty to be encouraged, like investigating whether giving out lollipops on test day improves SAT scores—but we may want to allow teachers more autonomy to follow their battle-tested instincts about what methods foster deep learning and understanding of materials.

The same story is reflected by the evolution of the Picbreeder *Skull* in Chap. 3. Without a diversity of users following their own varying ideals within the space of pictures, it is unlikely an image like the *Skull* would ever be uncovered. Perhaps the US Department of Skull Breeding would have more chance of success if they allowed different researchers to devise and follow their own measures of *Skull*-ness, instead of having one gold standard. Or better yet, if they allowed researchers to follow their own intuitions about what might lead to the *Skull*.

Of course, the insight is not that encouraging diversity can solve any particular ambitious problem—that would only be falling into the myth of the objective from a different angle. Instead, the lesson is that silencing diversity is a sure-fire way to slow down progress. So ultimately we're left with the conclusion that uniformity may be as meaningless an ideal as accuracy, especially when you have a specific ambitious problem in mind like improving education.

When it comes to education, we're essentially trying as a society to search for effective approaches to educating people. This problem is so complex and many-sided that great one-size-fits-all solutions have eluded us for decades. At this point, the natural question is, what does non-objective thinking imply for education? The critique so far in this chapter follows by now a familiar pattern—an objective approach falls prey to deception, leaving traditional assumptions about how to make progress on life support. But also familiar by now is that there's once again a silver lining if we manage to escape thinking only of the objective: Maybe sometimes teachers or school systems *should* follow their gut instincts even if assessments go down for a couple years. But that kind of gut instinct is discouraged with increasing objective pressure to "teach to the test" and improve scores. The result is to strip away much of teachers' autonomy, intuition, and creativity, slowly draining what made them passionate about teaching in the first place [60, 75].

Perhaps the effort invested in assessment would be better spent on trying different ideas without so much emphasis on accurate measurement. That would allow teachers to make use of their creativity and intuitive expertise, which they've honed through years of interacting with students. Like in Picbreeder, some of the resulting ideas might be destined for failure and others for valuable discoveries, but the *system* (in this case society as a whole) benefits from all the divergent paths taken at the same time. Those approaches that look interesting or promising then become stepping stones from which other efforts can depart. Through this process society becomes a treasure hunter for teaching methods. But this kind of healthy exploration of possibilities is stifled by today's rigid, objective-driven culture, at least in the US. (The primary education system in Finland for example provides greater individual autonomy to teachers and imposes no standardized tests on students [76, pp. 47–48]. In that sense Finland's system follows more the spirit of non-objective search. Finland also is a world leader in education, significantly outperforming the US [76].)

It's also interesting that higher education in the US, which only recently is being subjected to the same kind of "accuracy-based accountability," has long been considered world-class, while primary education, long the subject of unified objective efforts, has notoriously lagged behind globally. Sometimes being too objective is dangerous.

One frustrating aspect of critiquing objective-driven pursuits is that the alternative can seem hazy. But by now this moment of disbelief and doubt is familiar. In this book we've often arrived at similar moments as we examine great endeavors and wrestle with the false compass of objectives. Eventually we reach a point where there's no clear alternative to the status quo. The rebellion was fun while it lasted, but suddenly we long for the familiar comfort of objective thinking. The problem is that once we see the fundamental flaw in objectives, we're ejected into a wildly uncertain world and lose our usual bearings. So at least striving for higher objective performance, accuracy, and uniformity provide *some* bearings for improving education, even if they're faulty.

But once again there's a simple truth that can push us past the fear: We don't need objectives to find great things. We don't need to seek top performance or perfect accuracy to discover something amazing. It's like when we traded objectives for novelty in Chap. 5—we weren't left without principles, but with *different* principles that better reflect how discovery really works.

And the key principle to keep in mind is that the alternative to objective deception is the treasure hunter. And the treasure hunter is about collecting stepping stones. So when we're dealing with societal efforts like education, we might be able to make good progress if we as a society help expose each other to potential stepping stones to new ideas. In fact, rather than assessment, perhaps the best way to organize teaching is as a giant treasure hunt for the best approaches.

So how could we do that? Just as an example, imagine that most teachers and schools stop administering standardized tests to their students. Instead, at the end of every year, each teacher creates a portfolio of assignments, tests, syllabi, teaching philosophy, methods, and samples of student work. This portfolio is sent anonymously to a review panel of five other teachers chosen from different schools all around the country. The members of the review panel then assess their colleague's work on several measures, such as curriculum completeness, innovation, and student performance. These assessments include both ratings and written commentary. The teacher later receives the five anonymous assessments after they're completed. If the average rating across the different measures is lower than some failing grade, then *and only then* next year's class might be forced to take a standardized test to ensure some level of competence. Otherwise, the assessment stands for itself. While it might seem strange to rail against one kind of assessment and then immediately promote another kind, what we're critiquing isn't assessment itself, but the particular flavor of assessment currently in vogue, the kind tied to pursuit of ambitious objectives.

From the perspective of avoiding deception, the appeal of this peer-driven assessment approach is that people and schools are not being compared to *where we want them to be* (which is the objective fallacy), but rather are assessed based on *where they are* (which is the philosophy of the treasure hunter). What's most important is that the whole system is turned into a treasure hunter because it becomes entirely focused on spreading ideas around. Instead of being forced to converge to a soul-sucking teach-to-the-test approach, teachers are continually exposed to a diversity of ideas and approaches. This exposure happens because each year teachers are both serving on several panels and receiving their own assessments from other teachers. As a result they're constantly seeing the results of other teachers' approaches and are learning in detail the rationales behind them. That way, in the next year, they can try out the best of what they heard the year before and expand upon those approaches—which means jumping to the next stepping stone. The treasure hunter is set free, quality is still enforced, teachers can be creative, and the kids spend less of their lives immersed in endless standardized testing.

There are no easy answers in education, and we don't pretend to offer anything resembling a "solution" here. The point rather is to show how efforts as large and important as education can suffer from the same kind of mistake that leads robots into cul-de-sacs in Chap. 5, and that alternatives *are* conceivable. While it's unpleasant to admit that perhaps there's no objective approach to teaching everyone every skill we wish they had, it's really no different from pointing out the myth of the objective for any ambitious pursuit. Great things are accomplished in the long run not because they were the objective, but because they were not. For those who wish to enforce progress, this insight is demoralizing; for the rest it can be liberating. The next chapter continues in this spirit of liberation with an examination of objectives and their damaging effects in the pursuit of *innovation*.

Chapter 8
Unchaining Innovation

I tell you: one must still have chaos within oneself, to give birth to a dancing star.

Friedrich Nietzsche

On five ships, Magellan led over 200 men as they set sail from Spain in August of 1519, seeking a route to islands rich in valuable spices. Three years later, arriving on a single ship, the remaining 18 sailors who didn't starve could say that they were the first to circumnavigate the globe. But what they couldn't say was that they were even paid their full wages, because the profit from their cargo was so little! And Magellan himself was not among them—he caught a bamboo spear in his arm and was killed while raiding an island near Cebu [77]. A decade later in 1528, Giovanni da Verrazzano met a more grisly end. Although history remembers him as the first European explorer to sail into New York harbor, the price for fame was steep—he was killed and possibly eaten by natives while exploring an island in the Lesser Antilles [78]. Of course, the heavy risks faced by trailblazing explorers aren't unique to the sixteenth century. Hundreds of years later, after narrowly missing out on being the first explorers to reach the South Pole, Robert Falcon Scott and his men ran out of food on their attempted return to civilization, tragically freezing to death [79].

The stories of early explorers grab us. There's something enthralling about the raw danger and untapped potential of the unexplored. Driven by curiosity and promises of riches and glory, the intrepid explorers of yore went toe-to-toe with the unknown—and many lost their lives in the process. But those who penetrated the unknown (and returned still breathing) helped to expand the horizons of human knowledge. Now, with modern all-terrain vehicles, helicopters, and satellites, nearly every square mile of the world has been neatly cataloged and mapped. But beyond geography, there remain important unknowns left to challenge those still willing to explore: those unknowns within the space of ideas. And the benefits from human innovation can overshadow wealth or glory. In fact, new ideas and technologies have the power to reshape our world and society entirely. Following our exploration of the educational system in the last chapter, this chapter investigates how the myth of the objective also affects our pursuit of innovation, whether in science, business, or even art.

© Springer International Publishing Switzerland 2015
K.O. Stanley, J. Lehman, *Why Greatness Cannot Be Planned*,
DOI 10.1007/978-3-319-15524-1_8

Because scientific progress is currently so prominent in our culture, we'll begin with it. To make the case for the importance of scientific innovation, it helps to take a step back. Sometimes we forget how quickly the world is being transformed through scientific progress. A quote attributed to George Washington reveals a predicament we might find comical today: "We haven't heard from Benjamin Franklin in Paris this year. We should write him a letter [80]." Life in the eighteenth century was strikingly different from today's modern lifestyle, although the 300 year interval between them is a only a wink within the 40,000 years of human history. For a more recent example, Joel recalls his grandmother's story of how his grandfather courted her: "Well, for two years after World War II, your grandpa performed relief work in Paraguay, helping to build up sanitation. We corresponded by letters – mostly handwritten – and it would often take two weeks for one of his to reach me." Only two generations later, cross-continental real-time video chats through the Internet are unremarkable (and free!). It's amazing how scientific progress can transform our lives and what is possible. That kind of progress results from modern-day explorers who spend their lives probing *scientific* unknowns.

Of course, stories of scientific explorers working in laboratories or crunching numbers on laptops don't make for thrilling action movies. They may not evoke the same romantic sense of wonder as stories about braving storms on unfamiliar seas. But while scientists aren't eaten by cannibals and don't typically freeze to death when their experiments fail, the truths they uncover still hold real potential to turn the world upside-down. How would a universal cure for cancer impact society? What about cheap energy for everyone through nuclear fusion? So it may be no surprise that with such great potential, ambitious aspirations, and high stakes, human innovation has also become ensnared by the myth of the objective.

We often have a vested interest in scientific progress. Improvements in technology shrink the world, make our lives easier, and cure once-fatal diseases. So if scientific progress is slowed by objective obsession, it hurts everyone. But to see the impact of objectives on scientific progress, it helps to look at how science works in practice. Naturally, the most basic motor for science is provided by scientists performing experiments. But such experiments are often expensive. As a result, money is often the limiting factor for science—especially because advancing knowledge doesn't always pay in the short term. This means that scientists seeking to explore must first find *funding* for their projects. And it turns out that the sources of these funding decisions are often strongholds for objective-based thought.

But science funding is a different animal from education, the subject of last chapter, and as a result the way that objective-based thought manifests itself is different, too. One main difference between science and education is that we would never be happy with a school that is a complete and utter failure, but in science it is commonplace and expected for individual projects to fail. However, while there will be many individual failures, overall we'd like to expand scientific knowledge as much as possible. The problem is that there exist more scientific projects than can possibly be paid for, which means that risk and reward must be carefully balanced. That's why a critical question is, what principles should decide what scientific projects are funded or not? It's critical because poor decisions could hold back the the advancement of science, with enormous potential societal impact hanging in the balance.

From a high level, it's easy to see where deception might lie with respect to science: It's intuitive that scientific projects might seem like wiser investments if their investigators laid out clear objectives in a line and declared exactly what ambitious discoveries they will find at their completion. But the lesson from Picbreeder is that the most interesting discoveries can't be predicted in advance. So there's reason to believe that as in education, non-objective (i.e. divergent) thinking may also shed light on problems in how science is currently funded. Once again, advancing science serves as an interesting example of a different kind of societal objective than in last chapter's focus on education—it's an area where exploration is *essential* but individual failures aren't as dangerous. This kind of activity should be particularly appropriate for non-objective exploration. Still, we'll see that even in situations where occasional failure is okay, we often remain tied down by the myth of the objective.

$$*\qquad\qquad *\qquad\qquad *$$

In many countries including the United States, most scientific research is supported by grants from government funding agencies. Such grants are critical to advancing basic science because they support research that isn't yet commercially viable. Of course, it goes without saying that much scientific research won't pan out. Groundbreaking ideas are often also risky. So while some may succeed, many others will fail. This fact means that granting agencies like the US National Science Foundation (NSF) [81] or European Science Foundation (ESF) [82] must take some risks to have the hope of furthering the most innovative ideas. It's interesting then to examine how science funding agencies decide what to fund—because once again we'll run into objectives.

Scientists apply to funding agencies with a proposal that explains their idea. The proposal is then sent to a panel of expert *peer reviewers* who are usually respected scientists in the proposal's subject, like biology or computer science. Each reviewer gives the proposal a *rating*. For example, such ratings might range from *poor* to *excellent*. In general, those proposals that receive the highest average rating have the best chance of being funded.

At first glance this system looks reasonable. The best ideas in science ideally should be able to convince a panel of scientists that they're excellent. But there's trouble lurking behind the apparent common sense—the main effect of the system is to reward *consensus*. In other words, the more the reviewers *agree* that the proposal is excellent, the more likely it is that the agency will fund it. The problem is that consensus often works directly *against* exploring stepping stones.

For example, in Picbreeder, the reason so many images have been discovered is that users *don't* agree on which images are better. Picbreeder works as a stepping stone collector because each user can follow his or her own path, even when others disagree with that path or wouldn't take it themselves. But because there's no requirement for consensus, a Picbreeder user can leave any stepping stone she finds interesting, and others may later follow it to new places. Imagine if instead on Picbreeder a panel of "experts" voted on which picture to choose next. Compared to how Picbreeder works now, nearly all available paths would be closed off.

The problem is that when individuals with opposing preferences are forced to vote, the winner often represents no one's ideals (which perhaps explains the nearly-universal frustration people have with politics). Seeking consensus prevents traveling down interesting stepping stones because people don't agree on what the most interesting stepping stones are. And resolving this kind of disagreement often leads to a *compromise* between opposing stepping stones. Like a faded gray that results from mixing the sharp contrasts of black and white together, the product of such compromise often dilutes the two original ideals. For the scientist writing a proposal, the result is that the best way to win a grant is to propose the perfect compromise, the *best* faded gray—good enough to satisfy everyone, but unlikely to lead anywhere highly novel or interesting. So when consensus is sought in exploration, the result is a generic washout effect. Instead of allowing each person to discover their own chains of stepping stones, the system squashes a diversity of opinions into a generic average.

Perhaps then it would make sense sometimes to reward *maximal disagreement* instead of *agreement*. It's possible that *anti-consensus* may be more interesting than bland agreement. After all, attracting a unanimous vote in science could be a sign of nothing more than echoing the status quo. If you're doing whatever is hot and parrot the right buzzwords, you might be able to attract wide support. On the other hand, an *interesting* idea is likely to split votes. At the border between our present knowledge and the unknown are questions whose answers remain uncertain. That's why the opinions of experts should *diverge* in such uncharted territory. It's in this wild borderland between the known and the unknown that we should want our greatest minds probing, rather than within the comfortable vacation-spot of maximal consensus. Just think, which project is likely more revolutionary, one that receives *excellent, excellent, poor, poor*, or one that receives *excellent, excellent, excellent, excellent*? Splitting experts may be more of an achievement than unifying them.

Note that we're not suggesting that all-around poor proposals should be funded. If experts all agree that an idea is terrible, as in *poor, poor, poor, poor*, then there's no evidence that it's worth pursuing. But when *experts* radically disagree with each other, something interesting is happening. Darwin's theory of evolution was dismissed by many experts when it was first introduced [83]—a good sign! Thomas Kuhn spoke of paradigm shifts in which the present framework of science begins to crack. At those moments discord is the mark of revolution [84]. For all these reasons, some of our resources should go towards rewarding *disagreement* rather than consensus.

This argument ties into objectives because rewarding consensus is based on objective thinking. In the objective view, the more that experts agree that a path is worth taking, the more likely we should take it. The agreed path is an *objective* choice because people agree with its *destination*. The amount of agreement among experts provides a measure of the *best* destination—it's a kind of objective evidence.

If you seek convergence to the same ideas, then consensus is certainly an ally. That's why in objective-driven searches the focus is always on the ultimate *destination* rather than on the interestingness or novelty of the present stepping stone. So it can't be a treasure hunter. Only in non-objective search is the idea of unifying on a single destination discouraged. Only then can being *interesting* attract resources and funding.

Recall the difference in search between following the scent of interestingness as opposed to following objective performance. Science is among the greatest explorations of humankind—that we would reward primarily consensus in deciding where to step next is as stifling to discovery here as in any creative endeavor. No one is suggesting that *only* disagreement should be funded, but some of our resources should support the interesting over the objective. Science needs to be a treasure hunter and a stepping stone collector.

Of course, consensus makes sense for some kinds of decision-making—but not for creative exploration. And so the problem with consensus isn't limited just to science. Consider how in Picbreeder each user has the opportunity to pursue a unique path without interference from others. Even though someone else might later jump off from where a previous user left behind, never in the process is any consensus struck—and never is it needed to make discoveries. Sometimes the best path to creative ideas is to explore as individuals, without consensus or objectives. Later others can extend the ideas of their predecessors, keeping the chain going.

It's not that humans are bad at working together—on the contrary, the users on Picbreeder could be said to make an excellent team. It's just that they often work well in separated chains of discoveries rather than in consensus-based groups. But we're not suggesting that all scientists should work in isolation. Rather, the point is that disunity among research groups and within science as a whole can actually drive progress. In this way, disunity's power can help us better structure scientific and other creative endeavors.

                    *   *   *

Besides driving towards consensus, there are other ways that objective-based thinking can influence scientific funding. For example, if you believe in objectives, you might also think that the structure of scientific progress is predictable. In other words, the myth of the objective assumes the stepping stones to important discoveries are laid out in an orderly way. In this way of thinking, it might seem that the key innovation for curing cancer will likely be an improvement on a previous cancer treatment, or that at least it will come from research directly related to cancer. Yet time and again in this book we've seen that the stepping stones to remarkable results aren't predictable. So grand projects to cure particular diseases through direct focused research may not always be the best approach—if you actually want to cure that disease. However, even if such focused research fails in its original aim, as a byproduct it may enable unintended breakthroughs in seemingly-unrelated areas.

In fact, many grand projects of just this type have been undertaken by governments determined to solve particular problems through huge sums of research money. For example, in 1982, Japan's Ministry of International Trade and Industry initiated a massive decade-long research project called the "Fifth Generation Computer Systems project [85]." The project's aim was to propel Japan into world-wide leadership in computer technology. Despite all the money spent on a specific directed research plan, it's generally considered to have failed in its goals to create commercially successful products—although it did produce a new generation of promising Japanese researchers. Similarly, the "War on Cancer," initiated in 1971 by President Nixon with the aim to eradicate cancer as a major cause of death, has yet to succeed, despite targeted research to develop more effective cancer treatments and attain deeper understanding of cancer biology. Indeed, unrelated scientific projects like the Human Genome Project currently seem more promising for enabling better cancer treatments.

Of course, sometimes ambitious scientific programs can be successful, like the race to the moon in the 1960s, initiated by a commitment by President Kennedy: "I believe that this nation should commit itself to achieving the goal, before this decade is out, of landing a man on the moon and returning him safely to the moon and returning him safely to the Earth [86]." But this was an uncertain pronouncement that only proved possible because it was just at the edge of current technological possibility (that is, it was one stepping stone away when it was conceived). The chain of inventions that preceded the shuttle and made the shuttle possible were not part of the space program itself, although it depended upon on them. For example, setting the same objective in the 1860s would most certainly have led to failure.

The potential for misleading conclusions on the power of objectives to be drawn from such successes often fuels naive objective optimism, assuming that any objective can be set confidently at any time in history as long as sufficient resources are behind it. For example, a past president of the American Cancer Society once remarked, "We are so close to a cure for cancer. We lack only the will and the kind of money and comprehensive planning that went into putting a man on the moon [87]." Finally, even for successful cases of ambitious scientific endeavors, the most impactful resulting technologies for society tend to be unforeseen. For example, the space race yielded innovations like cochlear implants, memory foam mattresses, freeze-dried food, and improved emergency blankets.

Although these kinds of grand projects are easy to recognize and are clearly objective-driven, there are more subtle implications. A similar line of thought is that there is predictable structure in how scientific projects will *impact* the world. That is, maybe it's possible to optimize towards projects with *breakthrough* impact by consistently funding projects that currently seem to offer the most potential for impact. The idea is that moderately impactful projects will lead to even more impactful projects, and eventually to science that profoundly changes the world.

In this way, another objective drive in scientific funding is judging projects on the *importance* of their predicted *impacts*. In fact, a main criterion for evaluating grant applications in institutions like the NSF is the the broader impact of a proposed research project. As a result, projects perceived to have less potential for impact are less likely to be funded. The same sentiment is behind the tendency for politicians to mock research projects with seemingly whimsical goals as examples of wasteful spending—research that will clearly lead to nothing of importance. For example, a report by Senator Tom Coburn in 2010 summarized one experiment as "monkeys get high for science [88]," and another report in 2011 caricatured another experiment as "shrimp on a treadmill [89]." Similar in spirit were the monthly "Golden Fleece" awards given by US Senator William Proxmire from 1975 to 1988 to mock what he judged as obvious wastes of government spending. Award winners included scientific studies with evocative titles such as "The Sexual Behavior of the Screwworm Fly," "Behavioral Determinants of Vegetarianism," and "Motorist Attitudes Towards Large Trucks [90]."

The reasoning underlying these examples is the tempting idea that it's possible to classify research projects and their results as important or unimportant, as having wide societal impact or not, even before they are undertaken. Perhaps at this point in the book it is becoming evident that this idea is too simplistic—many important discoveries are serendipitous or unanticipated. As a result, predicting impacts is not always possible, and the attempt to do so *discounts* serendipity's important role. But even if it were possible to look at most projects and reliably estimate their impact, it still wouldn't be wise only to fund the most important ones.

The problem once again is that it can be short-sighted to judge an individual stepping stone by a criterion better suited to the whole system. Ultimately the aims for science as a whole are to uncover deep and transformative truths—but it may not matter at all if any particular project is transformative. In fact, it may be better that a scientific project is interesting and suggests further interesting and unanticipated experiments as a product, rather than it being at all important itself. The same is true of Picbreeder. As a system, it produces images of faces and cars even if individuals users cannot reliably do so themselves. And it's the same story with novelty search. As a system it may discover a robot able to reach the goal, but it only works when robots are not graded by their individual ability to reach the goal.

So if we accept that the stepping stones in science are unpredictable, like they are in Picbreeder, education, or any other complex undertaking we've reviewed so far, then "importance" is also likely to be deceptive. Does a moderately-important scientific result necessarily lead closer to a revolutionary *breakthrough*? Put this way, importance is just another broken objective compass: The stepping stones to the most important scientific discoveries may not themselves seem important, and the stepping stones to the most transformative technologies may reveal no hint of transformation themselves.

For example, many researchers in pure mathematics have no intention of ever impacting the real world, and their crowning theories often sit for years as purely intellectual achievements. The famous mathematician G.H. Hardy once called practical applications "the dull and elementary part of mathematics [91]," in contrast to the poetry of pure mathematics (which seeks truth without regard to application). Yet, despite the best efforts of pure mathematicians, these "useless" results often later end up supporting developments in physics or enable practical computer algorithms. Although created for purely mathematical purposes, a particular branch of abstract algebra called group theory nonetheless has practical applications in both chemistry [92] and physics [93]. Deep mathematics also provides the backbone for secure online commerce through public-key cryptography [94], which relies on the mathematical ideas of one-way functions and computational complexity theory—motivated entirely without online shopping in mind.

Another idea related to promoting grand projects or judging science by its predicted impact is funding science by its *alignment* with specific interests. Without getting too political, this often relates to a government wishing to promote only research agendas that it deems important at the time, or that provide clear short-term benefit to the country.

For example, the "High Quality Research Act" proposed by Representative Lamar Smith in 2013 states that before funding any project, the director of the NSF must publish a statement certifying that the project: "(1) is in the interests of the United States to advance the national health, prosperity, or welfare, and to secure the national defense by promoting the progress of science; (2) is the finest quality, is ground breaking, and answers questions or solves problems that are of utmost importance to society at large; and (3) is not duplicative of other research projects being funded by the Foundation or other Federal science agencies [95]." The assumption behind (2) is that judging projects by their importance is possible or desirable, while (1) assumes that it is possible to advance research narrowly along only the directions with direct benefit to the country, without searching more broadly.

While this particular act does not appear likely to be enacted in the United States, in Canada similar policies have been implemented. In 2011, the National Research Council (NRC) in Canada began shifting its research funds towards economic development at expense of basic research [96]. NRC president John McDougall explained that eventually only 20 % of the total budget should be spent on "curiosity and exploratory activities." And in 2013 the NRC declared itself "open for business," and consolidated its efforts into twelve "industry-themed entry points [97]." The NRC is "rebuilding itself to help grow Canadian industries ... all with the end goal in mind: high-quality jobs, increased business R&D activity, greater commercialization outcomes, and a prosperous and more productive Canada [97]." The clear shift is in moving away from basic blue sky research, and towards research aligned narrowly with the country's objectives. The important point is not inherently political as much as it is a general warning about the dangers of applying wishful objective-based thinking to ambitious scientific aims.

Naturally, it's appealing to think that large amounts of money can be reliably transformed into fundamental progress in specific important research domains. But the problem with narrowly aligned research and grand objective-driven projects is that whether the underlying idea is appealing or not, the structure of science just doesn't work that way. Who knows where the next great commercializable technology will come from? While this outlook may sound pessimistic, it makes the world of science a much more interesting place. Because while there are many elegant and important discoveries left to uncover, unearthing them requires constant ingenuity and openmindedness rather than simple brute force.

So it's not that scientific progress is impossible in general, it's just that we don't know what exactly will lead to important discoveries. Like the surprising value of disunity in science, there may also be wisdom in funding seemingly unimportant—though clearly interesting—scientific experiments. Though it likely requires passing through many unrelated steps first, following interestingness instead of narrow ambition may better reveal the stepping stones to transformative science and great economic growth.

As usual, you might ask how we can so smugly idolize stepping stones without knowing where they lead. But that's just the fading whisper of objective thinking. As we've seen, there's good reason to believe that not knowing where we're going is perfectly fine—and can actually lead to a brighter future of discovery. Not knowing where we're going is the way of the information accumulator, it's the treasure hunter, it's the stepping-stone collector, it's the path to everywhere and nowhere, it's the tunnel to the future. We don't know where we're going and *that's* why we produce great things. Consensus, perceived importance, alignment with national interests—these are "objective" parachutes for escaping the great unknown when we should be rocketing further into it.

*   *   *

Just as the value of disunity or unimportance might sound strange, objective-driven systems often sound sensible on the surface. For example, in the funding of scientific research, another objective aspect is that reviewers rate proposals based on how likely they are to succeed. In other words, the proposal must state its objectives, which the reviewers then assess. Many proposals are rejected because their aim is declared unrealistic or unclear by the reviewers. But given that objectives are often a false compass in any case, maybe the idea of *success* shouldn't always be the focus. The point is that not all projects should need to specify an objective, or even a hypothesis. Some research should be pursued simply because it's interesting, even if it's entirely unclear where it may end up.

We could even fund researchers with a track record of interesting discoveries in the past with no questions asked, like how MacArthur Fellowships grant a large lump sum to highly creative people. Of course, where these people's ideas might lead them is unclear, which might make you feel uncomfortable about giving them a blank check. After all, we don't know what they plan to accomplish or how they hope to do it. But the whole *point* of research is to go places that are unclear. If we don't accept that, then every serendipitous path without a clear goal is off-limits from the start. And as we've seen, ambitious objectives almost never work out. So forcing researchers to state objectives will cause the smart ones to propose only modest objectives, because those are the only ones that can realistically be assured—the ones that are but a single stepping stone away. Some readers will detect a hint of Paul Feyerabend in this argument—he taught that science can't be distilled to any one objective methodology [98].

One of the main reasons we tend to stick to objectives in general is a fear of *risk*. While some level of risk is necessary for progress, at the same time those paying the bills generally don't want so much risk that resources are simply being wasted on crackpot projects.

But our fears can't change the fact that risk is essential in science. The whole point is to cross many stepping stones over the long run. Because the hope is to travel far, risk-averse objective thinking limits and constrains progress. On the other hand, in areas likes business investing, the hope is for more short-term payoff. When considering innovative businesses, most investors recognize that the only good objectives are on nearby stepping stones. The point is, in the business world, it's often *also* a good idea to follow the interesting, but when the idea is presented to investors, it needs to be clearly reachable from the current stepping stone. So the innovative solution must be discovered *before* approaching the investor. To see what we mean, ask yourself which of the following two companies is a better investment:

1. **Holographic Television Manufacturer.** Forget about high definition, digital TV, or even 3-D displays. This company will invent 100 % immersive televised holography. You'll literally be able to walk through fantasy forests inside your living room. Unlike with current 3-D technology, it will be possible to circle around objects and see them from different angles. The entire television industry will be disrupted and entertainment will never be the same.
2. **Next-Generation Television Manufacturer.** The plan for this company is to increase screen resolution and image quality, bringing a better experience and value to consumers. Recent advances in display technology make possible this next step in quality.

While the objective of the first company is more revolutionary, few would put any money into that kind of scheme. There are plenty of arguments for avoiding the holographic TV company, but one of the biggest is that at some level we all know that holographic TV is many stepping stones in the future. When our personal savings are on the line, few want to bet on ambitious objectives because most of us share the instinct that merely setting an objective offers little guarantee of achieving it. The potential for deception is just too great to make such a risk worthwhile.

But the objective of the second company sounds a lot more realistic because it actually *is* one stepping stone away. *Realistic* objectives, which tend to be the province of *investing*, tend to be exactly those that are one stepping stone away. This fact is reflected in how most people invest—a solid business plan guides us only to the next stepping stone. But that doesn't mean that business can't be innovative—an *innovative* business idea reveals a nearby stepping stone that we didn't previously realize was there. The innovator in business also searches for the interesting, but waits to present anything to investors until the unexpected stepping stone is fully understood.

For example, how many predicted that advances in commodity consumer electronics would lead to the first mass-produced fully-electric sports car, the Tesla Roadster? Yet by bundling together what are in effect thousands of lithium ion laptop batteries, it became possible to create practical electric cars that were both lighter and more powerful [99]. There's nothing like suddenly realizing that we're one stepping stone away from some yet unrealized potential. Achievements once impossible snap into range through a previously unseen connection. What can be more exhilarating than discovering that air travel suddenly makes possible space travel, or that vacuum tubes make possible computation? Incremental steps into the blind alley of the unforeseen can reap huge rewards. On the other hand, there's little to celebrate (for the scientist *or* the businessperson) in simply committing to build the far future today. Sure, full-featured immersive holographic television sounds great, but good luck inventing one in the present. The stepping stones are yet to be discovered. In the end, the businessperson tends to look for nearby stepping stones before seeking funding, while the scientist ideally requests funding to follow a hunch that an interesting stepping stone is nearby. In neither case is setting a long-term ambitious objective the best choice, while in both cases innovation comes from the unexpected.

In the long run, it's the accumulation of stepping stones that leads to the greatest innovations. When each small step is a revelation, the chain itself is nothing less than a revolution. So while betting on revolution may be dangerous, over time it does happen. But as with all great processes of discovery, the revolutions are rarely the objectives of the stepping stones that lead to them. Investors recognize this principle even if it's not explicitly stated. In short, if you're looking to invest in visionaries, find those who wander in nearby shadows.

                    *   *   *

There does happen to be one group of innovators who already at some level grasp the myth of the objective. For *artists and designers*, the concept behind an idea is often more important than the goal (if there even is a goal). Art is more often about creative exploration than about satisfying a particular concrete objective. Ask an artist and he'll say it's better to follow inspiration's winding trail than to set out with the objective of painting the next Mona Lisa.

Of course, when art and design collide, such as in architecture, objectives do sometimes play a role. The roof has to keep the rain out. The foundation must be stable. It turns out there's an interesting parallel here between these kinds of "objectives" and the constraints on organisms in natural evolution. Every organism in nature must live long enough to survive and reproduce. But there are a multitude of divergent ways to meet this "objective," reflected in the vast diversity of life on Earth. From tulips to trees to tarantulas, life is creative within its constraints. So in a similar way, rain-proof roofs and stable foundations in architecture are more like *constraints* on creativity than typical objectives that are pursued for their own sake. Just as all organisms must reproduce, so in architecture must the building be functional and safe. Innovation in these worlds usually means finding new ways to respect the same old constraints that were present from the beginning. So even though the constraints do matter, the overall search is still driving towards uncharted spaces. (And if evolution interests you, this topic is discussed in greater detail in the first case study after the book's conclusion.)

It's easy to find dramatic examples of serendipitous chains of stepping stones in the history of art and design. For example, in painting, Impressionism led to Expressionism, which led to Surrealism. But the last thing that Impressionists like Claude Monet in the 1870s were worried about was how to trigger a Surrealist movement 50 years in the future. Still, the realistic depiction of light in Impressionist painting gave way to Expressionists like Henri Matisse who instead emphasized color and emotion. Eventually, as Expressionist painting became more abstract, it yielded yet another unexpected treasure—Surrealism, perhaps best known through Salvador Dalí [100]. The point here isn't to review art history, but to show that great new directions in art are often uncovered precisely because they were not the artists' objective.

Some steps on this road are rejections of previous steps while others are refinements or distortions. But the important point is that no one knows or plans their masterwork by trying to predict at the outset what those future twists and turns may hold. Each innovation is interesting in its own right, regardless of where it leads. At the same time, the potential to lead *somewhere* even more novel is often the tell-tale sign of healthy innovation. Expressionism wasn't captivating just for the paintings crafted in its style, but for the future possibilities it created.

But while we see that these principles hold across art's evolution in general, individual artists might not always recognize them. In 2011, Ken visited the famed Rhode Island School of Design (RISD) to talk about the danger of objectives to creativity. He was surprised to find many young student artists confused about how to *justify* their favorite projects. One student specialized in beating metallic surfaces with an axe and then rusting them on the beach after a dip in the salty water. He noted that he never knew what to tell people who asked him *why*. Even artists can feel the pressure to explain the purpose behind their works.

This question of purpose hides a common assumption: There must be some kind of objective to provide a *reason* for engaging in a particular creative act. To Ken's surprise, many art students told him that after his talk (on the subject of this book) that their trouble explaining their goals, which had previously provoked insecurity and doubt, now made sense—the greatest explorations have no goals. There's no need to justify taking an axe to pristine metal and later rusting away its sheen. The result is beautiful and thought-provoking. Such artwork is not only valuable for the way it suggests past violence and mellowing, but also for new related art forms it may inspire in the future.

If even artists suffer the pressure to provide objectives for their works, what more for the rest of us? It's a testament to the power of objective thinking in our culture that young art students would be hesitating on their path simply because they can't say where it leads. As the last two chapters have shown, the idea that progress is driven primarily through rigorous objectives affects everything from education to science to art. The way we organize most of our endeavors can't seem to escape the false comfort of objective thinking.

We hope we don't sound like we're offering the universal solution to every great problem. That would be naive, and far too grandiose to take seriously. Rather, what we hope you gained is an appreciation for just how omnipresent objectives can be. Their tentacles entangle every facet of our lives. From the most critical societal initiatives to the more mundane rituals of daily life and even the milestones of youth, objectives run almost everything. They're not always wrong, and even when they are wrong replacing them is no simple matter. But by seeing how they shape our view of the world and its potential, at least we can highlight that there is sometimes another way to think or to approach life. It *is* possible sometimes that the entrenchment of stagnant ways can be escaped by abandoning their false security. In some cases, the power of non-objective discovery and divergent exploration could indeed create a better future. And though non-objective search itself is not a universal solution, we're still better off seeing with sober eyes that slavish faith in objective exploration and assessment is often a formula for mediocrity and conformist stagnation. Although the world doesn't work in easy ways, at least we know that there's a path not limited by the shackles of a mandated outcome.

The last chapters have given us a taste of the freedom that's possible by escaping the myth of the objective. In the same way, the two case studies found after the book's conclusion also explore natural evolution and the field of AI research through the lens of non-objective thinking. Of course, we don't claim to have solved all the greatest problems. Education isn't yet perfect; science funding will never be a science itself; natural evolution still offers mysteries to be solved; and AI remains a distant goal. But while these challenges still stand, we hope you share our excitement in how non-objective thinking can change how we look at all of them. Perhaps this kind of liberated thinking can help us move forward. It may be just the stepping stone we need. In this hope, we conclude the book next with thoughts on accepting the loss of objectives as we know them.

Chapter 9
Farewell to the Mirage

Don't aim for success if you want it; just do what you love and
believe in, and it will come naturally.

David Frost

At this point we've covered a lot of evidence that objective thinking can hurt many of our society's most important efforts. Everything from the way we encourage the young to how we choose what science projects to fund suffers when objectives are overemphasized (and we've seen they often are). By considering new, open-minded approaches that discount the importance of objectives, we've suggested new practices in activities ranging from education to personalized automobile design. It's interesting and perhaps even inspiring to imagine what more might be accomplished if the grip of objectives on these kinds of important endeavors was loosened. But you might still question what this new non-objective perspective means for *you* personally. How might it change your own lifestyle as an individual? Objectives may be a myth, but what can replace them? It's fun to play the rebel and attack what is always taken for granted, but truly saying goodbye to a familiar habit is no easy task.

When you think about abandoning objectives, it might seem particularly difficult to follow through because no one wants to wander aimlessly through the world. Without objectives, the only remaining options might appear random or pointless. In this context, you might think that doing nothing might be just as good as trying your best. But that would be to misread the deeper implications of this book. All of us have an uncanny instinct for sniffing potential wherever it might lead. That very human skill does not require an objective, which is why freeing ourselves from this objective straitjacket does not mean living life randomly. On the contrary, it should give our lives new meaning. As a capstone to this book, we'll complete our journey by examining just what freedom from objectives really means for all of us.

Before we take this final step, it's important to recall that all along we've been talking about *ambitious* objectives. No reasonable person would suggest that all objectives should be wiped entirely from the Earth. Of course many objective-driven endeavors must and should proceed, and nothing in this book should contradict that. Houses should still be constructed according to the blueprint, software should still be designed to meet its specification, and there's no harm in following the

© Springer International Publishing Switzerland 2015
K.O. Stanley, J. Lehman, *Why Greatness Cannot Be Planned*,
DOI 10.1007/978-3-319-15524-1_9

recipe when you cook your next dinner. You might even increase your endurance
if you pick up running. All of these are modest objectives and not the target of the
arguments in this book.

The time when we might want to change our behavior is when we begin
to trespass beyond the familiar, when the hope is for greatness, discovery, deep
insight, or radical innovation. The quest for cures, elegant theories, beautiful structures, brilliant machines, soul-stirring melodies, epic tales, unfettered creativity,
travel beyond the stars, national healing, passionate release, true happiness—these
are places where objectives lose their power. When we seek out there, beyond
the horizon, where stepping stones fall silently behind shadows, that is where
the objective compass begins to quaver. And the farther out we go, the more the
objective becomes a deceiver, holding us back from our deepest potential—which
is exactly where it starts making sense to change our approach.

In case you think that sounds pessimistic, the startling fact is that revolutionary
achievement *is* still possible. This would be a very different book if its only message
was to stop being ambitious. But clearly we shouldn't stop. Evolution *did* discover
incredible organisms composed of countless intricate cells, humans did invent
machines beyond the wildest dreams of our ancestors, and even Picbreeder users
discovered images that no objective-driven program has been able to rediscover.
Instead of being pessimists, we just need to embrace *how* such discoveries are really
made, and what we can do to keep making them.

As we've seen throughout this book, the answer turns out to be a kind of
paradox—that we can find them by not looking for them—but that doesn't mean
that all is hopeless. On the contrary, it's critical to realize that just because you
don't *start out* searching for what you ultimately find does *not* mean that you are
necessarily searching blindly. For example, if you discover an ancient artifact while
exploring an uncharted river, it's not by complete chance—you found it because you
were exploring, even if you didn't know what you would find. So you can still search
by following principles, even if you aren't following any particular objective. The
only concession we have to make is that we can't be sure *what* we'll end up finding.
In other words, our destination becomes unknown. We have to concede *control* of
the final destination.

But the truth is this isn't really such a big concession anyway because that
supposed control was just a mirage. As we've seen over and over again by now,
although objectives are supposed to be instruments for controlling where you end
up, when they're overly ambitious they offer little more than the *illusion* of control.
They're actually more likely to become instruments of deception, leading us down
dead-end paths. So while it may feel that we're being asked to give up something
sacred, we never really had it anyway. No great breeder could intentionally steer
evolution from single-celled organisms to multi-billion neuron brains, no matter
the time allowed. No Stone Age genius could build a computer, and no modern-
day master could build a time machine. Clinging to grandiose objectives like those
offers no real escape from the unimaginable complexity of the search space, that
great unknown. The winding stepping stones along the path to the future are beyond

our ability to predict. When people do actually achieve amazing feats, they almost always build upon eons of accumulated innovations during which the final outcome was *not* the objective.

If you think about that fact, then conceding control of your destination is like throwing away an emotional crutch. There never really was a compass to great discovery or to ambitious outcomes. Perhaps that's why those who do succeed brilliantly are often cloaked in mystery and rewarded with devoted respect. We must at least have had an inkling that our compass is broken, or great achievements would not so easily become mythology. The objective is often little more than a good luck charm hung around our necks. That's why we don't have to mourn its passing.

In this spirit we can embrace searching without objectives confidently, because there really is no alternative. The only thing left to figure out is, once we give up believing that we can control our destination, what principle should we follow instead, and how can we put it into practice? The answer is to become the *treasure hunter*. Out in the vast wilderness of the unknown are countless treasures buried deep in unmarked locations. All these treasures are worth finding even though none of them may be something you're seeking in particular. But if you're lucky enough to find one, it comes with a bonus—a map of clues pointing to even more treasures. That's the stepping stone principle—one good idea leads to another. Treasures lead to more treasures, chaining and branching out across the infinite stepping stones of possible discoveries. So what you need to do is become a skilled treasure hunter.

For that to happen, you have to learn to search for clues. But instead of clues that the objective is nearby, they are clues that *something* is nearby that may be worth finding, like a mysterious but sweet aroma hanging in the air. This kind of clue can take many forms. For example, we saw that the novelty search algorithm considers novelty a clue towards future potential. Something new can lead to something even newer.

This strategy has worked surprisingly well in computers because novel behaviors (such as in robots) actually do seem like good stepping stones to more novel behaviors. A robot can't come up with anything much more interesting than bumping into walls unless it learns to avoid walls. So novel behaviors require learning some principles on the way forward, like what a wall is and what a door is. The result is that novelty-searching robots become more sophisticated as they try more behaviors. They can learn to travel through doors though it was never their objective. The point is that novelty search is a good example of a treasure hunter—it pushes towards new discoveries without any overarching goal.

Of course, humans aren't computers. Unlike the robots, we already understand *why* bumping into walls isn't going to get us very far. So we can apply this kind of understanding to our behaviors in a way that novelty search can't. To put it another way, our tastes are more refined than only craving novelty and nothing else. Of course everyone likes novelty in healthy doses, but there's more to life than that. That's why when humans become good treasure hunters, we like to mix novelty with something extra. While different people might describe that additional ingredient in different ways (perhaps you have your own idea what it is), one clue to it might be *interestingness*. It's true of course that we don't all agree on what's interesting, but as we saw even with Picbreeder, society ultimately benefits from people having diverse opinions. And interesting can mean a lot of things, whether it's a love for something like music or writing, or a desire to explore the world. The important thing is that the scent of interestingness can lead each of us across our own chains of stepping stones. As with novelty, one interesting thing leads to another. Where they will lead can't be predicted, but as long as we follow that scent, something worth finding is almost certain to turn up sooner or later.

That isn't to say that interestingness and novelty are unrelated. Ideas do become less interesting as they become less novel. There was a time when the concept of a self-propelled box on four wheels that transports passengers was radical. But these days describing the idea of a car at the next party you attend is unlikely to arouse much excitement. And "Horseless Carriage" likewise is probably not the best title for a new science fiction novel. Ideas that were once novel soon become familiar and mundane. But interestingness still goes beyond novelty. The sense each of us has of what is interesting is delicately tuned by our instincts, experiences, and knowledge. It might not be easy to explain exactly *why* a particular idea or choice feels interesting, but our unique human experiences are still behind that feeling. No computer program today can compete with this powerful human instinct for the interesting. And every interesting discovery we make can lead to even more interesting stepping stones in the future.

So if you want to be a treasure hunter without a specific objective, then there is a special kind of clue—when something feels *interesting*. That may sound simple, but the lesson behind it is deeper. It means that you can go treasure hunting by following your instinct for the interesting, not because you know where you're going, but because you feel the potential in where you are right now. Even just *accepting* that this treasure-hunting approach makes sense is important. It opposes so many of the messages we receive today from our culture that say you *need* an objective to achieve anything worthwhile.

Just consider how often we're asked to justify our actions against the supposed ideal of "being objective." If your boss or your parent thinks the justification for your choice is "merely" subjective, it will take a strong argument to escape that accusation. And what one person perceives as interesting is easily pegged by others as subjective. The fact that there are so many ways to criticize such choices highlights how easy it is to dismiss them: They're *unscientific*, *unprincipled*, *biased*, *emotional*, or even *irrational* or *irresponsible*. You aren't going to win over your boss simply because your idea *feels interesting* to you.

But the irony you can take from this book is that following just those kinds of gut feelings is often arguably *more* principled than being objective, especially when pursuing discovery or innovation. And this argument is not merely based on our feelings or personal preferences. Maybe it could have been dismissed as mere feel-good speculation if it were presented in isolation. But we've now seen an entire book of examples in which ignoring objectives led to better results than following them. Of course there will always be exceptions—some objectives are more modest and others may sometimes require objective-based assessment. But the point is that following the scent of interestingness *is* justified precisely because we don't know the structure of the search space. There is no way to know what new discoveries or ideas will later enable. They could be stepping stones to anywhere.

When you're standing on the edge of possibility looking out over the unknown, objectives become false beacons, but interestingness is different. Interestingness forms a network of roads leading from one treasure to another. The needles in the haystack pop into view only when we pause to appreciate the promise of the moment—the current stepping stone and the nearby stones to which it leads.

Contrary to popular belief, great inventors don't peer into the distant future. A false visionary might try to look past the horizon, but a true innovator looks nearby for the next stepping stone. The successful inventor asks where we can get from *here* rather than how we can get *there*. It's a subtle yet profound difference. Instead of wasting effort on far-off grandiose visions, they concentrate on the edge of what's possible *today*. At any moment in history, humanity possesses a specific set of capabilities and knowledge. This set contains all of our sciences, our technologies, and our arts. By combining some pieces within this set or altering them in a new way, one more capability can be added to the pile, and progress inches forward. The contribution of the true innovator is to take this baby step by noticing what is interesting in the here and now.

There are delicate moments in history when our set of capabilities steps over an invisible line and exciting new possibilities snap into view. Only those who are particularly perceptive and attentive notice the subtle change. For example, computer programmer Markus "Notch" Persson realized in 2009 that a new kind of video game was possible through combining concepts from three recent games: "Dwarf Fortress," "Roller Coaster Tycoon," and "Infiniminer." Unlike nearly all modern games, his resulting lo-fi game, "Minecraft," has outdated graphics, few frills, little content, and provides players with no explicit goals. Instead, players are free to discover, build, and create in a pixelated massive open world composed of cubes and recombinable resources. Few would have predicted that such a strange game could be successful, let alone that it might fundamentally alter the video game industry. Yet Notch understood the value of a new concrete possibility: Melding recent game innovations together could result in a new video game that was much like an interactive digital version of Legos, the children's toy [101]. Despite flaunting the usual conventions of big-budget modern games and having no publisher or advertising, the game has been a massive hit: Millions of players continue to craft and share remarkable artifacts, including functioning digital computers (that can play simplified versions of Minecraft itself [102]!) and intricate replicas of landmarks like Disneyland and the Colosseum—it's even become a platform for education [103]. What's more, in 2014 the game was sold to Microsoft for 2.5 *billion* dollars.

Similarly, when Apple Inc. first released the iPad tablet computer in 2010 no similar device had ever been successful. But within months *millions* were sold. As the leader of Apple, Steve Jobs had noticed that both society and technology had progressed to a point where a commercially viable tablet became *possible*. He wasn't distracted by overly ambitious visions of futuristic technology. He didn't pour effort into building sensationalist humanoid robots or human-level artificial intelligence. He could have, but that's not what he chose to pursue. Instead he saw the treasure in the moment, just barely coming into view from one stepping stone away, and he was the first to take the step. Interestingly, Jobs himself told a great story of the value in following the interesting without worrying about long-term objectives:

> If I had never dropped out, if I had never dropped in on that calligraphy class, then personal computers might not have the wonderful typography that they do. Of course it was impossible to connect the dots looking forward when I was in college, but it was very, very clear looking backwards [104].

In contrast to Notch's and Apple's success, objective-driven companies often dwindle without a product for years or decades. Without naming names, the commercial side of AI is littered with ambitious corporations who had to lower expectations. Many were founded on the vision of achieving some revolutionary new kind of AI. The difference between those kinds of disappointments and the success of Apple illustrates that deciding where to go based on *where you are* is often wiser than deciding where to go based on *where you want to be*. All of us can transform the present into the future. None can transform the future into the present.

That isn't to say that ambitious objectives can never be achieved. Sometimes frustrating old objectives do suddenly slip into range after sufficient ideas and innovations accumulate. For example, flying machines were an ambitious objective for centuries before the Wright brothers achieved flight. But it's easy to be misled by this kind of story because the failed attempts of the past are often driven by objectives, while the real reason for later success is different. In the past, and even into the time of the Wright brothers, those who pursued flight were primarily motivated by the inspiring vision of claiming the skies. Interestingly, Samuel Langly, their primary rival, attracted significant government funding to match the ambition of his effort, compared to the meager self-financing of the Wright brothers. But the Wright brothers had a different kind of motivation. In fact, they were originally bicycle manufacturers. It turns out that for them bicycles were stepping stones to flying machines. You could say that they saw in the present an echo of the future, rather than trying to drag a preconceived vision of the future into the present. So while flight was an objective for many failed visionaries over hundreds of years, it was when the bicycle-makers realized that planes are bicycles in the sky that it actually happened [105]. The moral is that just because an ambitious objective is ultimately achieved does not mean that it was realized *because* it was an objective. To believe that would be to believe in the myth of the objective.

Letting go of objectives is also difficult because it means letting go of the idea that there's a *right path*. It's tempting to think of progress as a set of projects, some of them on the wrong path and some on the right. If you see the world this way, it's natural to defend the path you believe is right and to confront those who seem misguided. But here's the strange thing: When there's *no destination* there *can't be a right path*.

Instead of judging every activity for its potential to succeed, we should judge our projects for their potential to spawn more projects. If we really behave as treasure hunters and stepping stone collectors, then the only important thing about a stepping stone is that it leads to more stepping stones, period. The worst stepping stone is one that leads nowhere beyond itself, no matter how nice it may feel to stand upon it for the moment. As treasure hunters, our interest is in collecting more stepping stones, not in reaching a particular destination. The more stepping stones we find, the more opportunities there are to depart to somewhere greater.

Judgmentalism is the natural habitat of the objective-seeker, always worried about where everyone else will end up. But we are all better off in the end if we end up at different places. Otherwise, everyone would be standing on the same stepping stone. That's why we need to beware of the seduction of consensus. Of course, if we all want to end up in the same place, the *right* place, then it makes sense to push towards consensus. But that should be the last thing we want. Disagreement and divergence are virtues that deserve to be protected. What is the real danger of someone disagreeing with your path aside from ending up in a different location?

Of course it can't be denied that some efforts are destined for more success than others. But the world is too complex and too diverse to know for sure where we should all head at this moment, which just means that life is very deceptive. And that's why it's valuable to society to allow different people to take different paths and let the stepping stones fall where they may. Not every stepping stone leads easily to another. Some will even be dead ends. But objectives open even fewer possibilities, pointing in only one direction at a time.

Imagine the poverty of a Picbreeder on which all its users were searching for a butterfly. Not only would there be almost nothing interesting on the site, but the crowning irony is that there would probably be no butterfly either. We need to be careful not to model society in this misguided form.

So if you're wondering how to escape the myth of the objective, just do things because they're interesting. Not everything needs to be guided by rigid objectives. If you have a strong feeling, go with it. If you don't have a clear objective, then you can't be wrong, because wherever you end up is okay. Assessment only goes so far. A great achievement is one that leads to more great achievements. If you set out to program computers but you're now making movies, you're probably doing something right. If you wanted to create AI but you're now evolving pictures, you're probably doing something right. If you imagined yourself painting but you're now writing poetry, you're probably doing something right. If the path you're on does not resemble where you thought you'd be, you're probably doing something right. In the long run, stepping stones lead to other stepping stones and eventually to great discoveries.

It's exactly those kinds of chains of innovation that make the best achievements possible. But to achieve them strangely requires letting go of them. It's hard to let go, but just remember that the lost objective may still return someday, years from now, when the right stepping stones are laid. Until then, we can follow the scent of interestingness, of novelty, or of whatever present clues we feel may propel the great treasure hunt of innovation. You don't have to give up every objective in your life, but if you want to achieve greatness, if you want to explore the blue sky, if you want to travel past the horizon, then yes, in some cases you will need to abandon them.

In today's culture, it's rare that we follow this kind of path. The prevailing philosophy is to *chain* exploration, to enslave it to our objectives. But the evidence suggests that search works best when it is a treasure hunter. We can avoid the temptation of convergence and instead unleash the ever-branching treasure hunter. It's in your interest that some do *not* follow the path you think is right, because one day *they* will build the stepping stones that lead to your greatest discovery.

When all is said and done, when even visionaries grow weary of stale visions, when the ash of unrequited expectation settles on the cloak of the impenetrable future, there is but one principle that may yet pierce the darkness: *To achieve our highest goals, we must be willing to abandon them.*

Chapter 10
Case Study 1: Reinterpreting Natural Evolution

The nucleic acids invented human beings in order to be able to reproduce themselves even on the Moon.

Sol Spiegelman

Every one of the many cells that make up your body is bustling with activity. The mitochondria power plants hum along, burning sugar to keep the cell going. The ribosome factories pump out whatever proteins are needed to repair the aging cell membrane or build new structures. The lysosome garbagemen mop up the waste from the factories, and the local government housed in the nucleus maintains order by enforcing its DNA constitution. And despite all that's going on, it's easy to forget we're made of cells at all.

But each cell in your body is an incredibly intricate microscopic machine—each a kind of miniature city in its own right. What's amazing is that everything about you results from fifty *trillion* of them working together as a well-coordinated team. To put that number into perspective, there are ten thousand times more cells in your body than there are people living in the world. If that isn't mind-boggling enough, modern science tells us that the unguided process of natural evolution is what created and organized this massive team of cells that make us who we are.

Beyond even that, natural evolution designed *every* organism on this planet. Every one of us is related to each other through the sprawling tree of life. From the Hyperion redwood tree in Northern California, which is over 700 years old and 400 feet tall, to the archer fish in the waters of Indonesia that can squirt down an insect from nine feet away, all living things are our relatives. They're our cousins a billion times removed, because every organism shares the most distant great-grandparent: the very first replicating cell.

Normally when you study something, it's brought down to earth as you come to understand the mechanics of how it works. The connection between the low-level parts and the high-level functionality becomes clearer. A bike works because the pedals move the chain, and the chain moves the wheels, and as a result the bike rolls forward. And if you leave a bike alone for a million years, it will simply rust away.

Most things we know about are relatively boring in this way. They don't keep creating new, different things as products. But evolution is unique because it continually makes new from old, a kind of perpetual recycling machine. Unlike

© Springer International Publishing Switzerland 2015
K.O. Stanley, J. Lehman, *Why Greatness Cannot Be Planned*,
DOI 10.1007/978-3-319-15524-1_10

the bike, if you leave evolution alone for a million years, it can completely recreate an entire ecosystem. The more you study evolution, the more incredible it seems. How can it be that an organ as complicated as our own brain is produced by a mere *mechanical* process? It's precisely this kind of skepticism that fuels the *intelligent design* movement.

These skeptics argue that just as the fine craftsmanship of a Swiss watch points to a talented watchmaker, the diverse and complex creatures living on Earth must similarly point to a gifted (and intelligent) creature-maker. But Charles Darwin made an important discovery that undercuts this kind of argument. It turns out that a slightly-broken copying machine can lead to the *appearance* of intelligent design.

Imagine a copying machine that makes copies *of itself*. If the copies are exact, the machine might not be very exciting—you would just get a warehouse full of the same thing. The twist comes if the self-copies are slightly *imperfect*. The result of this kind of imperfect copying is that you'll end up with a *variety* of different machines, because each machine will make something slightly different than the last. Of course, some of these copied machines might be different in ways that destroy their ability to copy themselves. Or perhaps some copying machines over time will become bullies or resource hogs and actually *prevent* other machines from collecting the metal they need to make a copy of themselves.

The machines that don't make copies of themselves rust over time until they no longer work, leaving them no children to carry on their lineage. But in each generation, those machines that do copy themselves *would* have children that resemble them, continuing the legacy of the parent machine. This is the main idea of *natural selection* that Darwin uncovered—only self-copiers that succeed in copying themselves will be explored further by evolution. Together, inexact self-copying and natural selection produce an *evolutionary process*, a search for many different ways for slightly imperfect self-copying machines to exist together. And if you unleash this process for a few billion years, you get all the diverse complexity of life on Earth.

So in the end, we could say that Darwin discovered that the *process of evolution* is itself the mysterious creature-maker. In fact, there is very little reason to doubt the theory of natural evolution—unlike those who subscribe to intelligent design—because the scientific evidence backing evolution is truly staggering.

Still, because evolution is complicated and science constantly expands and questions itself, biologists don't fully understand *every* aspect of evolution on Earth. For example, the origin of life itself is still not entirely settled (although scientists have many good theories). Biologists also debate several different *interpretations* of evolution. This kind of disagreement isn't over what evolution *does*, but on how to *view* evolution, and what ingredients of evolution *cause* it to be so creative and powerful. In other words, different interpretations can disagree on which *forces* are most responsible for driving evolution. In particular, a key question is, how important is *natural selection*?

Natural selection is the idea that genes that allow an organism to have more children are likely to spread throughout the population of organisms. So in natural selection, genes that hurt an organism's ability to survive tend to disappear over time, while genes that enhance survival are likely to spread. Sometimes in popular culture it might seem like the phrase "natural selection" means the same thing as "evolution." But evolution is more than just natural selection. There are many evolutionary forces, and natural selection is just one of them. In fact, disagreements over the importance of natural selection compared to other evolutionary forces has led to some serious debates among biologists. For example, one of the most famous of these arguments was between Steven J. Gould and John Maynard Smith, both respected evolutionary biologists. Gould thought that chance and history in evolution were perhaps *more* important than natural selection, while Smith argued that natural selection was more important than chance [106]. So while both agreed that evolutionary theory is right, they disagreed over its *interpretation*.

Importantly, the interpretation we choose can influence how we understand evolution. Is evolution best understood as being driven by *optimizing* survival and reproduction through natural selection, or as a more divergent process that happens to *accumulate* different forms of life? The right interpretation can help us to understand how the remarkable outcome of the wide diversity of natural life resulted from an unguided process. In this spirit, this chapter explores an alternative interpretation of natural evolution—one inspired by viewing it through the lens of non-objective search.

As in previous chapters, one motivation for this investigation is to demonstrate how non-objective thinking can flip our perspective when thinking about creative discovery. But at the same time, the hope is also that re-examining evolution will provide a deeper understanding of it. Importantly, our aim isn't to overthrow settled biological theory. Instead, we're suggesting an alternative point of view, a different way of interpreting evolution that may help us comprehend *how* it's able to do the incredible things it does. But before introducing this alternative interpretation, first we'll review the most common ways of viewing evolution and why they're so strongly tied to objective thinking.

The most famous catchphrase on evolution is likely "survival of the fittest." In this slogan, "fittest" refers to the biological concept of *fitness*, which means how many offspring on average an organism tends to produce. But "survival of the fittest" isn't something Darwin actually said, and it's not a favorite of modern-day biologists either, who prefer the term "natural selection." Still, it's important to keep in mind that "survival of the fittest" is ingrained in the public understanding of evolution. And more than that, the phrase does a good job of capturing one driving force behind evolution: Creatures that are better adapted to their particular niche will tend to out-reproduce their less-adapted peers.

A gene that changes a rabbit's fur to neon-yellow would make it easier to spot by predators, which might hurt the rabbit's ability to survive. A gene like this probably wouldn't spread throughout an entire population of rabbits because those rabbits carrying it would on average produce fewer offspring. On the other hand, a gene that makes a rabbit faster may enable it to better escape predators and *increase* its fitness. In this case, the gene would likely multiply throughout the population because the faster rabbits would tend to live longer and have more opportunities to reproduce. So these genes, whether they cause neon-yellow coloration or faster bounding, end up competing with each other. As a result, the rabbits themselves are forced to compete because they're built from the blueprints of the competing genes.

This insight about competition helps connect "survival of the fittest" to objective thinking: The whole notion of a competition for survival suggests a competitive search for ever-more-fit organisms, which leads ultimately to the objective of "the fittest," or the best reproducer. We might hope for a more specific objective than simply "the fittest," but it's a start for thinking about what the objective might be. Like all objective-driven searches, a measure for performance is defined (in this case *fitness*) that aims for increasing improvement.

For similar reasons, "survival of the fittest" is also responsible for the popular view of natural evolution as a bloody competition among organisms. If only the fittest survive, then nature looms cold and cruel, extinguishing those organisms that fail to measure up objectively. As Tennyson put it, "Nature, red in tooth and claw." Focusing on competition in evolution leads to the outlook that nature always strives to improve itself; but—here is the interesting question—to what end? What objective is nature striving to achieve? Early evolutionists believed, and indeed many non-experts still believe that evolution is *progressive*, moving towards some sort of objective perfection, a kind of search for the über-organism. This interpretation sometimes places humanity as the current pinnacle of evolution. In other words, it might seem that from an evolutionary perspective we're *objectively superior* to bacteria or cockroaches.

But even thinking about evolution objectively leaves room for different interpretations. The most naive is to imagine that evolution is set up *explicitly* to search for humans as its objective. This kind of human-centricity can be seen in early depictions of the tree of life, where humans are prominently perched on the highest branch. The implication is that humans represent evolutionary progress. However, of course most biologists today wouldn't endorse such a human-centric view. In fact, if humans were evolution's explicit objective we'd end up with the now-familiar objective paradox: If every organism from the very first cell on Earth was selected for its similarity to humans, humans would never have evolved. As with any overly ambitious objective-driven search, the problem is that the stepping stones don't resemble the final product: Our actual evolutionary ancestors, such as flatworms, don't resemble us. So evolution couldn't have been actively searching for us— otherwise we'd never have been found! So if evolution *is* driven by a clear objective, it would need to be something other than just simply to create humans.

What could that objective be? One possible idea is that if humans weren't explicitly the objective of evolution, maybe a *trait* that distinguishes us from other living things was the real objective. For example, perhaps *intelligence* was the objective of evolution that led to humans. But the problem is that the same argument against ambitious long-term objectives still applies. The stepping stones to intelligence aren't intelligent themselves. For example, without the benefit of hindsight, it isn't clear that flatworms are a better path towards high-level intelligence than insects. But we didn't descend from insects. Having the foresight to see so many stepping stones ahead—from flatworms all the way to humans—is too much to ask from an unguided process. What we're really talking about once again is deception. Deception is the reason that it doesn't make sense to think of evolution as a search *for* humans, *for* intelligence, or for any other human-centric trait. The human-centric view just comes out implausible.

In fact, evolution is just one of many major scientific discoveries that took humans off our pedestal as intrinsically special. Copernicus demonstrated that Earth wasn't the center of the universe [107], Wöhler showed that the chemistry of living things wasn't separate from the chemistry of the non-living [108], and similarly Darwin discovered that humans were just one of the many leaves on the tree of life [109]. None of this of course undercuts all the amazing abilities and traits of humans, like our ability to share complex ideas or our exceptional intelligence. The real point here is that *evolution* doesn't treat us humans specially. There's no hint in evolutionary theory that we're elevated over any other creatures.

In any case, while we may not be evolution's objective, the question still remains, how could evolution produce something as intricate and intelligent as us? What, if anything, *is* the objective of evolution? The answer is important because it might help us to understand our own species' origin more deeply.

As we briefly discussed in Chap. 4, most people with a scientific background would say that *survival and reproduction* is evolution's objective. Let's now examine this perspective a bit more deeply. It's true that all living species share this ability to survive and reproduce—because if any species failed to survive and reproduce then it wouldn't be here. But above just surviving and reproducing, this perspective also acknowledges an evolutionary force driving towards *greater* survival ability: natural selection. So in this view, it is *improving* fitness (which is biological shorthand for the ability to survive and reproduce) that is often seen as evolution's objective. And natural selection is the main force driving this kind of improvement.

Importantly, natural selection provides an explanation for why organisms are so well adapted to their environments: Selection is constantly trying to improve how an organism fits with its surroundings, like a puzzlemaker trying to whittle a piece's edges to better fit with its neighbors. This insight is captured well by the words of evolutionary biologist Theodosius Dobzhansky: "Nothing in biology makes sense except in the light of evolution." By peering at the living world through the lens of natural selection, the mystery of design fades: Trait A is explained as having evolved to help organism B deal with situation C. This line of thinking might suggest that the deepest interpretation of evolution is that it continually strives to increase the fitness of all organisms. In short, evolution's objective is to keep increasing fitness. This view of evolution fits neatly within the objective paradigm and also makes intuitive sense. In fact, evolution is traditionally presented to us this way in school and an educated person would likely explain evolution similarly if asked. But in this book we've seen that sometimes *questioning* common objective-based explanations can lead to the deepest insights. So let's see if there's a different way to think about the diversity of life.

*   *   *

While "survive and reproduce" sounds at first like a reasonable objective, under further scrutiny it starts to show some holes. For example, recall that in Chap. 4 we considered that "survive and reproduce" doesn't fit what we usually mean by the word "objective." While debating the definitions of words isn't always the most interesting exercise, in this case it's important because the choice of words *gives life* to the explanation. Whether or not an objective explanation makes sense depends on what we really mean by the word "objective." And *survive and reproduce* is just not like a typical objective that we might face in day to day life, like finding a lost set of car keys.

Remember from Chap. 4 that a suspicious fact about *survive and reproduce* is that it was already accomplished when evolution started. The very first cell survived and reproduced. In contrast, it would be silly to search for car keys that you had already found. Finding something typically signals *achieving* the objective, not the beginning of a search. But evolution *began* in just this way, with an initial reproducing life form that already met its goal.

More deeply, if we view evolution not only as trying to achieve survival and reproduction, but as searching for the organism that survives and reproduces *the best* (that is, the most fit organism), then we're still left with contradictions. The problem is that this view clashes with deep intuitions about what makes evolution interesting. In particular, in a typical search it's usually the *end point* that is most interesting. For example, in a search for lost keys, the lost keys themselves are the main focus. If evolution is viewed as an objective search for the most fit, then the counterpart to the lost keys is the overall most-fit organism. And fitness is defined in biology as how many offspring an organism will produce on average. So if evolution is about increasing fitness, then it's a search for the organism with the highest fitness.

Here's where the problem comes in—which organisms tend to produce the most offspring? If a married couple has five children, we'd view them as pretty ambitious. However, five kittens are often found in just a single litter, and cats can have many litters. The unintended implication is that cats are objectively more interesting than humans. Even worse, bacteria are far more prolific than any animal. So then bacteria, which were discovered earlier in evolution, and which are much simpler than humans, must be closer to the evolution's "objective" than humans. But humans still cry out for an explanation. If bacteria are more optimal, what drove the search towards us?

Of course, it's not bacteria that we find most fascinating about evolution. So something is wrong if our view of evolution puts bacteria on top. Bacteria might be interesting, but the incredible diversity and complexity of life is far more profound than the smaller slice representing bacteria alone. Life's massive variety, including tortoises as well as tulips, cows as well as cowpox, sheep as well as seashells, couldn't result from something like a simple search for lost keys. Life seems more like the product of a collector's odyssey to accumulate all variety of keys, some of which are incredibly more sophisticated than others.

In fact, the diversity of discoveries in evolution should remind us of the other branching creative processes we explored in earlier chapters. Just as the flatworm was a stepping stone gathered by evolution without knowing that it would later lead to humans, so the *Alien Face* was published to Picbreeder without knowing that it would lead to the the *Car*. And so was the vacuum tube invented without knowing that it would someday enable computation. Evolution begins to look more like the unfolding processes of Picbreeder or human innovation than it does objective-based achievement. In this way of thinking (as noted in Chap. 4), when we look at the most inspiring achievements of evolution, such as photosynthesis, flight, or human-level intelligence, it's interesting that none were ever its objective. If we're interested in the *products* of evolution and want to understand how they come about, then considering evolution as a search for an objective is unhelpful. Fundamentally, the objective-based explanation dangerously ignores that the most interesting products of evolution become just a *side-effect* of the drive towards the objective (high fitness). It would be more elegant to have an explanation in which the products, the vast diversity of life, are *central* and not just a by-product of the main theory.

In this light, focusing on evolution's creativity instead of attempting to box it into the objective-based paradigm might lead us to a deeper understanding. It's misleading to apply the word "objective" to "survive and reproduce" in nature because it's so different from typical objectives in objective-driven searches. Objectives aren't usually satisfied the moment search begins, and objective-driven searches nearly always aim for what they ultimately produce. So with creativity instead of objectives in mind, where will it lead us to take a non-objective perspective and re-examine natural evolution in that light?

A different way to think about *survive and reproduce* is as a *constraint*. As always, organisms that fail to reproduce will go extinct, while those that do reproduce will persist. But this perspective allows us to flip the usual interpretation on its head: Rather than pushing progress ahead, perhaps selection actually *restricts* exploration. The fact that some organisms aren't selected to reproduce means that their potential to act as stepping stones will never be explored. In this way, thanks to selection, much of the search space is actually pruned away.

To illustrate this point, imagine a magical alternative Earth that's kinder than our own. Let's called it Gentle Earth. In this alternate reality, natural selection is removed entirely. There is no longer *any* competition, no need for red teeth or claws. In fact, in this gentler world, *every organism* is allowed to reproduce. Even those that wouldn't survive on their own receive help to ensure that their genes are passed on anyway. The idea is to completely remove the force of selection in this world. In fact, Gentle Earth is so forgiving that even organisms without sexual organs are made to reproduce anyway, even if it requires creating their offspring (who still inherit their genes) out of thin air. Overcrowding isn't a problem though, because Gentle Earth is suitably large to contain all the extra organisms that otherwise would not have been selected on normal Earth. The result is that many organisms that would never have been born through evolution on Earth (with selection) will get the chance to exist and reproduce on Gentle Earth (without selection).

Assuming that evolution starts with the same initial cell on Gentle Earth as on regular Earth, what would be the outcome of this experiment? You might first think that this sort of evolution would not produce anything interesting—because there's no pressure for organisms to *adapt* to their environment. Without adaptation, which is the usual explanation given by biologists for complex biological traits, there is no *need* for organisms to improve objectively. But is selection really necessary in the strongest sense to create the complex creatures we see around us? Or is it possibly a restriction that limits the creativity of evolution?

Assuming that the same mutations and matings occur on Gentle Earth as did on Earth, the remarkable fact about Gentle Earth is that by now, we would observe all the variety of life we see in the real world, *and much more*. As strange as it sounds, this outcome is certain because everything that would have passed the filter of natural selection *still* would survive on Gentle Earth as well. By eliminating the pressure of selection, it becomes *less* difficult to be considered for further evolution. In fact, on Gentle Earth there is no way for an organism to lose the chance for further evolution. So every offspring ever produced on normal Earth would survive to reproduce on Gentle Earth as well, which means that the same lineages would be explored. Of course, because literally *every* organism (including those that would not be viable on Earth) is guaranteed to reproduce, there would be a lot of uninteresting inanimate cellular blobs on Gentle Earth as well. But the positive side of this tradeoff would be that many interesting organisms that just happened to be unlucky and did not survive on real Earth would be given a second chance on Gentle Earth.

For example, imagine a rare once-in-a-million-times mutation that gives the beginnings of an exciting new ability to a newly-born organism. On normal Earth, before this intriguing mutant has the chance to develop, it might be eaten by a predator—forever cutting off what might have been an important discovery and a stepping stone to other interesting places. But on Gentle Earth this mutant is only the beginning. Gentle Earth is a much more open-ended explorer, leaving no stone unturned. Who even knows what kinds of unimagined body plans might arise without the need for an organism to develop and support genital organs? The point of this thought experiment is to illustrate that selection is *not* really a creative force: It focuses and optimizes, and ultimately restricts exploration. Selection's grand achievement is only to ensure that resources (which are finite on normal Earth) are spent on organisms that can reproduce on their own. And this kind of restriction isn't the same as exploration. So "survive and reproduce" can be viewed as constraining the stepping stones that evolution explores further, and not an objective in itself.

This shift in perspective exposes evolution as a classic treasure hunter instead of an obsessive optimizer. That is, one hallmark of natural evolution is how it accumulates novelty and diversity. In a similar way to how stepping stones accumulate in human innovation, in Picbreeder, or in novelty search, natural evolution accumulates different ways of making a living on Earth. The tree of life branches ever outward from the root, growing in scope as it proceeds, collecting new stepping stones as it goes. Not all the stepping stones survive, but those that do become links in a growing chain to new discoveries.

But what causes evolution to accumulate stepping stones in this way? The key element of evolution that generates its awesome discoveries is not just competition between organisms, even if competition may play an important role. The problem with competition as a general explanation for creativity is that it usually drives towards everything converging to the best. And the best is only one thing, not an endless series of stepping stones. For example, the NCAA March Madness tournament begins with 64 teams but ends with only one champion. While there were once a wide variety of competing paper clip designs—only one remains. In battles between Betamax and Cassette, DVD and Laserdisc, or HD-DVD and Bluray, one format eventually eclipses the others [110–112]. But natural evolution isn't like these kinds of competitions because it drives towards *divergence*, towards a multitude of varying solutions to life's problems. As in other examples of non-objective search, it's exactly this accumulating and branching through the space of stepping stones that leads to the most impressive discoveries.

Interestingly, it's not by competition that natural evolution leads to diversity, but often by *avoiding* competition. In particular, if an organism can make a living in a new way, then it has effectively founded its own niche. Because it then becomes the first organism to live in this new way, the competition is less intense for the lucky newcomer and it can reproduce more easily. For example, if a chance mutation gives a creature the ability to digest a previously inedible compound, it could claim a whole new class of food entirely for itself. Over time its descendants may specialize mainly to consume this new-found treasure, founding a new species as a result.

Or consider the revolutionary achievement of the first land animal ever to fly. This prehistoric Wright brother expanded into a new universe of possibility and escaped predation on the land. In this way, novel niches accumulate: While individual species may go extinct, it's rare for an entire way of life to remain unexploited for long. Nature is always seeking to expand.

Additionally, a new niche often makes founding newer niches possible, and such newer niches often lead to even newer ones. Like a chain reaction, new niches bubble up continuously from the old. One unappetizing example of how niches can multiply is given by the dung beetle: The waste products of one organism may become the food of another. Or a prey may offer new opportunity to a predator, as gazelles are often food for lions. Just as the invention of the computer formed the foundation of an entire ecosystem of software that couldn't have existed without it, the discovery of grass by natural evolution provides a platform for herbivores to make a living. Those herbivores in turn enable the carnivores that feed upon them, the scavengers that clean up the scraps, and the parasites who live within the animals themselves [113]. The chain reaction that the first cellular niche set off billions of years ago shows that evolution in nature belongs in the same club as human innovation, Picbreeder, and novelty search: Evolution is also an ever-expanding collection of stepping stones that build upon each other, not because they improve in any objective sense, but because they explore beyond the stepping stones of the past.

The similarity with other non-objective search processes doesn't stop with accumulating stepping stones. Serendipity also plays an important role in evolution, where it seems impossible to predict what one innovation might later make possible. Just as human discoveries are sometimes unpredictable, chance plays a pivotal role in natural evolution as well, most notably through mutation. A mutation is a slight copying error that sometimes happens when an organism reproduces. These errors often cause the small visible changes between a parent and its offspring, and are sometimes impacted by natural selection. If a mutation devastates an organism's fitness then the mutation will almost certainly disappear from the world quickly. On the other hand, mutations that don't much affect fitness have more uncertain fates, because natural selection will be mostly indifferent towards them. These kinds of neutral genetic changes evolve not by natural selection, but according to aimless *genetic drift* [114].

In particular, although natural selection channels chance to a species' advantage, sometimes there are attributes that natural selection ignores. If a given trait doesn't affect an organism's ability to survive or reproduce (for example, the color of an organism's bones), then natural selection will not direct that trait in one way or another, and its evolution will instead drift. In this sense, some diversity blossoms not because of selection, but despite it. In fact, the less selection is acting, the safer it is for drift to explore, as the biologist Michael Lynch has emphasized [115].

Another force that allows serendipity to act in evolution is *exaptation*, which occurs when a feature of an organism evolved for one function proves useful in an entirely different context. For example, birds' feathers first evolved in dinosaurs, where they helped to regulate temperature. Only later did evolution exploit them as a stepping stone to flight. Closer to home, the precursors to our bones merely stored minerals needed for other bodily functions. Later on, evolution repurposed them to give our bodies solid structure [116].

Stories like these are common in non-objective search, where stepping stones are not measured against far-off objectives to determine their survival. It's no surprise then that a process like exaptation also occurs in Picbreeder—remember the story of the *Car*, whose wheels were exapted from the eyes of the *Alien Face*. And exaptation is common in human innovation as well: The vacuum tube that was invented only to help in early investigations into electricity was exapted later to enable computation. In this way, exaptation is one of the key properties that empowers non-objective search. An intriguing pattern that we observe in many different kinds of search processes is that interesting discoveries for one purpose often to prove useful in the future in a variety of unexpected ways.

So it's possible to view the creativity of evolution not as the product of competition, but rather as *escape* from competition. When stifling constraints on survival are lifted, the search can plow uninhibited through the search space, drifting and exapting its way to new stepping stones. Through this force for diversity, evolution gradually accumulates novelty. It's just another non-objective process— what it ultimately produces was not set as an objective from the start—just like Picbreeder, human innovation, and novelty search. Though on the surface they seem different, the push for diversity in all these systems is aided by the non-objective stepping stone collector—the treasure hunter strikes again.

*   *   *

We can now begin to see how the popular interpretation of natural evolution as driven by competition may actually focus too much on evolution's least interesting feature. In other words, when we view evolution as a search for optimality or efficiency, we're equating it with more boring searches, like finding the most efficient route from your house to the library. Unlike in evolution, a definitive *best path* to the library can be found—and it will not lead to a branching tree of endless possibilities. The problem is that viewing evolution as a competitive search for optimal organisms suggests that evolution itself will someday converge to an ultimate uber-organism. But because the reality of evolution is more profound, focusing on creativity instead of optimization can refresh old thinking.

At the same time, it's important to avoid the inference that contrasting interpretations must be incompatible. While a new interpretation could imply that the earlier interpretations were *wrong*, in reality the same set of data can support more than one interpretation. So just being consistent with the data isn't enough to decide between competing interpretations. But how then should we choose between them?

In this case, the hope is to provide an elegant explanation of what is causing an observed process. A good interpretation should illuminate the *deeper meaning* of the raw data. The formula for the universal law of gravity is interesting, but the *explanation* behind it is more profound: Matter attracts matter, a simple and elegant truth. In the same way, an illuminating interpretation of natural evolution should capture the essence of how its awesome products are generated. Ideally the right interpretation would be so concrete that it could even inspire a new kind of computer algorithm. Imagine if we could bottle up the power of evolution and apply it wherever we like, to cars as easily as to robotic pets. It could serve as a kind of innovation machine that would continually spit out fascinating new artifacts. Leave this machine alone for a few hours and you could come back and enjoy a brand new type of automatically-designed car. The point is that interpretation isn't just an academic exercise. If the interpretation is clear enough then it can lead to insights so concrete that they can be formalized and applied to many other contexts.

An important tool in understanding natural processes is *abstraction*. The idea is to capture the essential features of the underlying process while discarding unimportant details. Abstraction cooks an idea down to its essential elements. For example, the concept of a checkerboard can be abstracted as an eight by eight grid of alternating red and black squares. It doesn't matter if a particular checkerboard features a blemish on one square, or if it's slightly longer than it is wide. These sorts of unimportant details don't impact the purpose of the checkerboard: to play the game of checkers. Abstraction wipes such inconsequential details away. The more we can abstract away while maintaining the heart of the idea, the better the abstraction is. Of course, the danger of abstraction is zooming out too far, to the point that even the most important details are lost. A checkerboard abstracted as only a big square would be overreaching in this way. While it's true that checkerboards are approximately square, the game of checkers can't be described with that perspective alone—playing checkers depends on there being 64 separate squares, not just one big one. The challenge with abstracting natural evolution is to boil it down to the most fundamental explanation of its creative power—all without throwing away any essential details.

A good place to begin abstracting is with the perspective that "survive and reproduce" is a constraint rather than an objective. An organism that survives long enough to reproduce will have its lineage continue onwards, while an organism that doesn't reproduce will act like an evolutionary dead end. By taking this slight but important step of viewing survival and reproduction not as the driving force of search but as a limitation on search, all successful organisms in evolution now become equals. In other words, we no longer care about how well an organism reproduces, how quickly, or even how it lives or is structured—we only care whether it does or does not survive and reproduce. The result is that in this abstraction successful organisms all effectively do *the same thing*. They all survive and reproduce. Interestingly, they can't *improve* in this respect, because even the very first organism could meet these criteria. Instead, all successful organisms do the same thing (survive and reproduce), but they do it in different ways. By leaving behind the familiar idea of fitness, this perspective opens a new window for explaining the process that really drives discovery in nature.

Nearly all organisms begin life as a single cell and pass on their genes to their offspring. And their offspring are also at first just a single cell. This single-cell "bottleneck," as Richard Dawkins calls it, is ubiquitous in nature [117]. It's interesting to look at evolution through the perspective of this bottleneck: It leads to the idea that nature has found an incredible diversity of methods to start from one cell to do nothing more than ultimately produce another. What happens in between is life. All animals are unified through this bottleneck although they may cross it in strikingly different ways. In fact there is a hint of *Rube Goldberg machines* in the awesome contortions taken by life to start from one cell only finally to produce another of the same type.

The simplest way to crack an egg is the most direct. You can just strike it on a hard surface. But there are other ways to do it too. You could build an intricate machine that performs a bunch of random tricks, each one triggering the next, before eventually cracking the egg with a mallet. If you've ever played the board game *Mouse Trap*, you're already familiar with these kinds of funny machines, which are known as Rube Goldberg machines (in honor of the cartoonist and inventor Rube Goldberg who pioneered them). In Mouse Trap, the players collaborate first to build an elaborate machine made of miniature elements: a crank, gears, a lever, a boot, marbles, a chute, a bathtub, a seesaw, a diver, a pole, and a mouse cage. The climax of the game is when the trap is triggered, and if it's constructed properly, a long series of events leads to a plastic mouse being trapped by a falling cage [118]. Of course, the cage could have been triggered in any number of more direct ways. But the signature of Rube Goldberg machines is that a simple task is achieved in an overly complicated way. In other words, the main result—triggering the mouse trap—is unimpressive when compared to the needlessly elaborate way in which it's achieved.

Complex organisms share this property. If all organisms begin their life as single cells and end up reproducing to create offspring who also start as single cells— and this simple strategy for reproduction is effective—what *objective* utility is there in doing the same thing, but in more and more complicated ways? Bacteria make the leap between generations of bacteria in a relatively simple way, like cracking the egg directly against a surface. But some organisms take a more roundabout path: They might first spawn a trillion excess cells and perform an elaborate well-choreographed Rube-Goldbergian dance for two decades. Finally, they will reproduce the next generation as single cells. Humans take this more roundabout path. In fact, a single sperm cell and a single egg cell united years ago to form the original single-celled version of you. And now, years later, you stand as a trillion-celled tower of reproductive inefficiency. When viewed this way, a human is curiously like a complicated outgrowth of a bacteria's reproductive process. We proliferate trillions of cells to produce our offspring where only one is needed to do the job.

What we're noticing here is that there's a difference between what we find *interesting* in evolution and what is only *necessary* to survive and reproduce. The most interesting developments are *digressions* from the objective of maximizing reproductive fitness. These digressions persist not because of competition but through other mechanisms in evolution (like drift and exaptation) that encourage creativity. Even though we create trillions of cells where only one would do, our evolutionary niche supports such unbridled extravagance, allowing the beautiful Rube-Goldbergian dance that we humans do.

There are many ways to meet the minimal criteria of life, whether a beetle, a bird, a buffalo, a barnacle, or a businessman. But when we view these diverse creatures from a high level of abstraction, they're all at heart doing the same thing—they survive and they reproduce. The difference is just that they do it in radically different ways. Instead of competition, in this view the engine behind evolution's creativity is *searching for many ways to do the same thing*. Evolution may be the original Rube Goldberg, endlessly riffing on the same simple theme.

But *why* would evolution search for many ways to do the same thing if there isn't a direct incentive to do so? Is there some other force pushing it? It sounds like a good question but there really doesn't need to be an explanation. An interesting thing about search is that a process that merely drifts gently through mutation from one generation to the next will diverge outward in the search space without any incentive. It's like starting at zero on a number line and adding small random numbers over and over again—eventually you would reach big numbers. It's as if someone spilled milk into the search space at the particular point occupied by the very first single-celled organism. Over time, the spill keeps spreading outward in every direction, filling the space of possibilities. The constraint of reproduction simply means that some areas of the search space, those representing organisms that can't reproduce, are barriers to the spill that will never fill. So evolution simply flows around the sterile and lame, filling up every point in the search space that can reproduce to lead to other points. In some places, the spill is accelerated by the discovery of new niches, opening new canals to further locations. Although much of the spill is passive and just drifts along with no particular selective pressure behind it, escaping from competition by founding new niches does reward novelty.

In this way, the novelty search algorithm described in Chap. 5 is like natural evolution with the accelerator pressed to the floor—*always* rewarding the most novel with more offspring. Today we're witnessing the result of an ancient spill that spread mindlessly through the space of all possible organisms that can reproduce. And like novelty search, when the simple ways to survive are exhausted, the spill simply trickles into areas that are more complex, because there are no other areas left to fill. Pour liquid for long enough and it will eventually fill a volume, stepping stone by stepping stone.

Seen this way, evolution is a special kind of non-objective search: a *minimal criteria search*. It isn't heading anywhere in particular, but it heads everywhere that passes the minimal criteria of survival and reproduction, which was satisfied from the very start of evolution by the first reproducing cell. Evolution is just accumulating all the different ways to survive and reproduce. And as all the simple means of living are exhausted by the search, gradually more complex ones are uncovered. But they aren't discovered because they are *better* or more optimal— they are simply the stepping stones reachable from where the search last stood. The minimal criteria spill just flows onward. Once again, it is *because* there is no objective that evolution is so prolific: An objective would simply cut off more of the search space. In fact, this insight that evolution is a kind of minimal criteria search led us to invent a variation on the novelty search algorithm, called *minimal criteria novelty search*. This new algorithm was able to produce robot behaviors that solve mazes that even novelty search could not solve: It did so by searching for maze runners that found novel ways to do the same thing [56]. What's interesting about this result is that it shows how high-level abstraction led to insights that could be tested as a practical automated spill-filling algorithm.

*   *   *

Of course, it's difficult to ignore that in this view competition has been completely abstracted away. This spilled-milk view of evolution is so high-level that fitness is abstracted as a hard constraint: Either you survive and reproduce or you don't. There can't be competition (like there is with fitness) with only a hard constraint, because any way of meeting the constraint is *equally good*. But as biologists would argue, competition *does* play a certain role in natural evolution, which this abstraction ignores. However, competition may be the least *interesting* of the evolutionary forces because it tends to *diminish* diversity. Unlike the accumulation of different ways of living that results from discovering new niches, competition isn't a purely creative force. It's more a honing force that optimizes creatures within a particular niche, or in limited ways across niches, like when gazelles adapt to run from lions. So if we're interested in the *creativity* of the process, it's not unreasonable to abstract competition entirely out of evolution. The problem with competition is that it introduces the concept of objective pressure to be better, which as we've seen can lead both to convergence and deception. Put another way, evolution is creative *despite* the competition it tolerates—not because of competition. For example, on Gentle Earth (where there is *no* competition) evolution would be even more creative.

So for evolution to produce impressive products it's critical that competition doesn't overpower the drive towards creativity. It's important that the task of surviving and reproducing in natural evolution is a general, open-ended constraint. As a result, it's solvable in many different ways. These different ways of living are achieved through the creative forces in evolution, including the drive to escape competition by founding new niches. Just as some Picbreeder users may have objectives and some may not, competition in nature doesn't stop the system as a whole from growing in diversity. It can hone these different lifestyles and may lead a particular niche to be dominated by a particular organism, but still new niches will continue to accumulate. The important conclusion is that even when abstracting natural evolution in a way that includes competition, competition should play a *secondary* role to creativity.

The sensible question then is how competition in nature takes on this less central role. Why does competition not cause natural evolution to converge to a single optimal creature? An important fact about competition in evolution is that it isn't *global*. In other words, each organism is not in competition with *every* other organism. Competition is restricted in different ways. For example, it's restricted geographically, such that birds in Australia don't compete with birds in America. Competition is also restricted by niche, such that birds in general don't compete directly with buffalo. Importantly, this restricted *localized* competition has a much different effect than global competition, which imposes an overarching global objective on the search: Global competition emphasizes uncovering the *best* overall. In global competition an organism would be judged by how it compares to all other organisms. A human being competing globally with bacteria on the yardstick of reproductive fitness would not measure up (the bacteria reproduce more often and more quickly).

Then how is local competition different? As first highlighted by famed biologist Sewell Wright, local competition crafts and adapts organisms within their own niches, but only produces limited effects *between* niches [119]. The result is that unlike global competition, local competition encourages the founding of new niches to *escape* competition. In discovering a new way to live that's free from previous competitors, competition is reduced—by running away from it. But in global competition there is no escape: No matter what an organism does it will always be judged against all others. That's why global competition naturally leads to convergence while local competition naturally enhances diversity and creativity. So the idea of (localized) competition can be folded into the non-objective abstraction: Natural evolution can be seen as a novelty-generating search with local competition.

Once again, this interpretation doesn't contradict biological fact nor suggest that biologists have been wrong. Instead, the idea is to recast evolution in a different light in the hope of deeper understanding. In fact, we also formalized this refined abstraction as another algorithm called *novelty search with local competition*, yet another variation of the novelty search algorithm. This algorithm balances creating novelty with competition while remaining non-objective and accumulating diversity. Interestingly, when combined with a virtual creature simulator, the algorithm produced a wide variety of virtual creatures in a single experimental attempt, something that hadn't been done before [120]. In this way the algorithm helps to confirm that searches of this type can yield fast explosions of diverse forms.

*   *   *

A key insight from thinking non-objectively in this chapter is that although evolution can be seen as a competition, out-competing other creatures on the "objective" of surviving and reproducing is less important than *escaping* from competition to form new niches. That's how diversity grows and why natural evolution overall diverges rather than converges. It's how stepping stones accumulate and the potential of the system as a whole ratchets upwards. Just as in other forms of non-objective search, it's when the reigns of optimization are thrown off that discovery finally takes over. A final interesting question is whether the fossil record itself provides further evidence for this non-objective view of evolution.

Evolution is remarkable because it's unguided. As a mindless process it can't plan ahead, or craft sophisticated objectives as humans do. So its successes cannot result from overcoming deception through intricate knowledge of objectives or from raw intelligence—because evolution is a purely mechanical process. As a result, natural evolution's great success *must* follow from its mindless accumulation of stepping stones, because that's all it ultimately can do. A striking feature of the tree of life is that it's always branching outwards as new niches and variations of existing organisms are uncovered. But these branches aren't leading anywhere in particular. All the fossils that archaeologists study don't point in a straight line towards some supreme accomplishment. They're all just different shots in the dark, slight unthinking variations of past evolutionary experiments.

The first known fossils date back about three billion years. Back then they were imprinted by single-celled organisms and loose colonies of cellular life that resemble modern-day bacteria. It's interesting to note the lack of *progress* since then: The dominant life-form, in raw number, and also in diversity, was and still are single-celled organisms [121]. Evolution means change, but this niche has been remarkably constant. Instead of forgetting the past and replacing it with something new, evolution remembers the past, not only in fossilized rocks, but in the single-celled living fossils that make up nearly half of the mass of all living things (despite their minuscule size) [122].

Though bacteria are still around, since their first discovery life has conquered a staggering variety of additional niches. Many of these niches involve growing larger or more complicated. Take for example the famous "Cambrian explosion" that occurred about a half-billion years ago (during the Cambrian period). This "explosion" was a particularly productive period in evolution when the precursors of all the modern animal groups evolved in a relatively short time span (a few million years) [123].

Before the Cambrian explosion, life was limited to small simple niches, similarly to how Picbreeder begins with simple pictures, or the behaviors of maze navigators in novelty search are at first simple, or human innovation starts with the wheel and not the internal combustion engine. In other words, the initial simple stepping stones must come before the more complex. The Cambrian explosion was just another stepping stone that natural evolution was exploring without any idea of where it would ultimately lead. You might say that it repeats the familiar story: the discovery of rock and roll, the invention of computation, the Picbreeder *Car*, and now even evolution's creation of body plans. From this point of view, we can see the fossil record itself as the original story of serendipity, written not with words but through dead organisms immortalized in rock, a billion-year testament to the rich power of the non-objective treasure hunter.

It's precisely because evolution has no overriding objective that it was able to discover something like humanity, precisely because it wasn't looking for us that humanity was found. The paradox of objectives unifies all large-scale open-ended creative systems—from human innovation that's driven by our own intelligence and exploration of the interesting, to natural evolution with its notable lack of human guidance or design. In the end we're left with a different perspective on evolution. It seems more similar to open-ended brainstorming than single-minded pursuit of a goal; more about exploration than about bloody competition; more like constructing novel Rube Goldberg machines than aspiring towards perfection. Evolution is the ultimate treasure hunter, searching for nothing and finding everything as it spills through the space of all possible organisms. It's the world's most prolific inventor. Even so, everything it ever produced was done without thinking about where it might someday lead. That's why it becomes possible to understand evolution largely without the ideas of competition and fitness, perhaps providing a new perspective that doesn't appeal to the myth of the objective.

Chapter 11
Case Study 2: Objectives and the Quest for AI

> *The only principle that does not inhibit progress is: anything goes.*
>
> Paul Feyerabend, *Against Method*

Not so long ago, the technologies we take for granted today were unimaginable. Even the richest medieval king still traveled by horseback and could easily die from pneumonia. But today even the average citizen can travel through the skies and communicate instantly with friends thousands of miles away. For all this—and much more—*science* can take the credit. At its heart, science is the search for knowledge. It expands what's possible and allows us to understand the world more deeply. And like in all great searches, the scientific discoveries of today are the stepping stones to the unimaginable technologies of the future.

While the march of science is often dazzling, its progress comes from the work of scientists, who are human and imperfect like everybody else. And because human beings are behind its great advances, the way they communicate and interact profoundly impacts science's rate of progress. It's important for us to understand how this system works because science shapes the quality of our lives. Just imagine life without antibiotics. So if the scientific community could work together more effectively, all of us would stand to gain. So let's take a look at the way science works today and discover whether troublesome objectives are lurking in the background.

First, science isn't really just *one big community* that includes all scientists. There's too much knowledge in the world for any one person to understand it all. As a result, scientists *specialize* in one or two smaller areas of scientific knowledge, called *disciplines*. Familiar ones include physics, biology, and chemistry. Each of these scientific disciplines is represented by a different community of scientists. Just like any other human community, these disciplines each have their own customs

© Springer International Publishing Switzerland 2015
K.O. Stanley, J. Lehman, *Why Greatness Cannot Be Planned*,
DOI 10.1007/978-3-319-15524-1_11

and culture. A lot of jokes play on the cultural differences in different scientific communities. For example:

> A Mathematician, a Biologist and a Physicist are sitting in a street cafe watching people going in and coming out of the house on the other side of the street.
> First they see two people going into the house. Time passes. After a while they notice three people coming out of the house.
> The Physicist: "The measurement wasn't accurate."
> The Biologist's conclusion: "They have reproduced."
> The Mathematician: "If now exactly one person enters the house then it will be empty again [124]."

While cultural differences in lifestyle between countries often relate to language or cuisine, cultural differences among scientific communities relate to expanding human knowledge. The hope is that a discipline's culture promotes fruitful exploration so that the most promising stepping stones in that discipline can blossom. At the same time, there's also a need to limit time invested in exploring dead ends. Because the time and resources of individual scientists are limited, it's important that each community helps its members to identify the most important ideas. That way, the scientists in the community can keep up to date without reading *every* paper ever written. That's why most scientific communities follow rules intended to weed out bad or uninteresting theories and experiments. You can imagine that without this kind of filter, the firehose of research produced by a community would be overwhelming.

To filter and spread the most important ideas, most scientific disciplines publish their work in journals and conferences. Journals, which are published on a regular basis, spread the ideas and results of diverse researchers. In contrast, academic conferences allow researchers to meet in person to discuss and share their work. The "proceedings" of conferences (a record of what happened there) are often published, and sometimes include all the papers that were presented. The main point is that publishing your ideas in journals or conference proceedings helps to validate your research and spread your ideas to the larger community. The ideas that are accepted for publication in journals and conferences are important because they shape the direction of future research—they're the stepping stones that tend to be explored further. So the interesting (and significant) problem is how best to decide which ideas should be published and which should be discarded.

The most common solution to this problem (also mentioned in Chap. 8 for deciding which scientific projects should receive funding), is called *peer review*. It begins when a scientist hoping to share a new idea with the community submits it to either a journal or conference. Next, the editors of the journal or conference proceedings don't simply read the article and publish it if *they* like it. That would be too much power for a small group of people to wield over the future direction of a discipline. Instead, the editors' job is to find *peer reviewers* that are experts in the area of the submitted idea, and ask for *their* opinions of it. These reviews are often detailed, and their aim is to highlight mistakes and judge how important the idea is. Later the reviews are collected by the editors and sent back to the authors, so they can revise their submission and improve it. Then the process repeats—with revision, resubmission, and another review. It continues until either the idea is accepted (and published) or flat-out rejected. The purpose is to ensure that the ideas that are published are accurate and important.

The hope is that peer review will reject or improve weak ideas, while the most important ideas will be published. Through publishing, these important ideas reach the top minds in the field—who can explore them further as stepping stones, and science can continue to march forward. But this system also creates several significant risks. It's possible that the "experts" chosen to review a particular submission might be biased or close-minded. They might see a new idea as a threat to their own theories, or fail to grasp what makes it interesting. The idea might seem to be too radical or it might clash with common beliefs in the discipline. On the other hand, the reviewers might recommend publishing unimaginative ideas that support the status quo—freezing innovation. And just as in other human communities, power and politics can poison scientific communities too. Powerful members might cause the review process sometimes to stray from fairness and open-minded ideals. So if a community isn't cautious, it can stagnate as the gatekeepers play favorites and hold back progress.

It shouldn't surprise us that somewhere lurking behind these concerns is the powerful force of objectives. Because they're concrete and allow progress to be measured and encouraged, people tend to like guiding any search or process of discovery through objectives—and science is no different. It's simply easier to demand the objective of a particular idea than to judge an idea without one. So when reviewers confront new ideas, it's natural that questions about objectives will come to mind: What will these ideas accomplish? Will they lead to a particular objective? But the habit of focusing on objective-driven questions in scientific communities can produce unintended results, just as with other objective-driven activities. So the role of objectives in science deserves a closer look. To get this new perspective, let's examine the thinking within a particular scientific community. Think of it as a case study to help us understand the effect of objective-driven thinking on science in general.

The artificial intelligence (AI) community is a natural choice for us as the authors because it's our own research community. But more than that, the AI community is especially interesting because its central focus is to reach a very ambitious objective: to create a machine or program that is highly intelligent. This orientation towards a far-off objective makes it easy to see the effect of objective thinking in AI, which might be more subtle in other disciplines. While it's true that the exact definition of AI can vary between researchers, in general, most who haven't lost their passion want to work towards something ambitious, like human-level intelligence or beyond. The point is that with AI we're talking about pursuing a classic highly-ambitious objective—a discovery still *many* stepping stones away.

Of course, this book has cautioned against any large-scale effort geared towards a far-off goal. Naturally this warning presents a kind of paradox for studying AI. The problem is that trying to head somewhere distant and ambitious is a fundamental part of the field of AI. Perhaps that's why it's popular for some AI researchers to hedge and say that they're just creating practical algorithms for the present day and aren't interested in some foggy far-off dream. But how can we avoid thinking about how a breakthrough in AI might result in truly intelligent machines, radically changing the world forever? Airplanes might fly on their own, robots might build houses—and design them too. Beautiful music might be composed by tiny chips without human intervention, and our future rescuers might be made of metal instead of flesh. All of this is possible if AI's most ambitious objectives are achieved.

That's why AI is a good model for looking at how objective thinking impacts science. It becomes a case study for how objectives affect communities in general, even those outside science. So the lessons of this chapter aren't only about the field of AI, but extend much further. After all, objectives are a favorite tool of society's *gatekeepers*—the people in power who decide where to invest resources and what to ignore. So not only will we learn about the inner workings of a particular scientific community, but about the role of objectives in social decision-making in general.

To understand the AI community, it helps to think about what researchers in AI make. In particular, the products of AI research are typically *algorithms*, the bread and butter of the field. No theory is complete, no idea confirmed, unless it's first written as an algorithm and then tested. This tradition keeps AI grounded—any wild claims can be tested with computerized experiments. Researchers have to back up their written arguments with real results.

Because one goal of AI is to build computers that perform useful tasks, there are a wide range of AI algorithms. There are programs that recognize objects visually, write their own fiction, control robots, play chess, learn on their own, and even play video games. Because any behavior that might require intelligence is fair game for AI, the algorithms in AI cover the full range of tasks performed by humans and animals. Of course, some behaviors are harder to achieve than others: A computer named Deep Blue defeated the human chess champion Garry Kasparov in 1997 [125] but today an algorithm that learns on its own to tie a shoe is still a great challenge. The Holy Grail for AI would be a single algorithm that can do everything that we can do—and perhaps much more. But this kind of algorithm—if it's even possible to write—is still a far-off goal, even as the field keeps moving forward.

Because algorithms are what AI researchers produce, the field of AI itself can be thought of as a *search for algorithms*. In other words, the community of AI researchers as a whole works together to search for new and better algorithms. And in a similar way, researchers in mathematics search for new theorems, and researchers in physics search for new laws that better describe reality. However, something interesting and unique about the AI community is that its researchers study *how* to search effectively. Scientists in AI are experts at designing AI algorithms, and many of these algorithms are *themselves* designed to automatically search through large spaces. For example, some AI algorithms search for the best path through a maze while others search for the best move in a board game like checkers or chess. So the twist is that the field of AI is itself a search for algorithms, and AI researchers are themselves experts on thinking about searching. In other words, AI researchers are *searching* for algorithms that search. There's nothing particularly mysterious about this, it's just that search is an important part of intelligence, so it's no coincidence that both human and artificial intelligence turn out to involve search.

As an example of how a search algorithm works, in the field of *machine learning* (which is a community within AI) an algorithm is often searching for the best set of parameters. In a typical problem, there might be many parameters that tell a program how to drive a car or control a biped robot (the biped experiment in Chap. 5 is an example of a machine learning problem). A search algorithm can search through these parameters to try and find the best settings for driving or walking—that way people don't have to waste many hours doing it themselves.

Some of these car-driving parameters might include how close to hug turns, how hard to press on the accelerator, and how much distance to keep from the car in front of you. Of course, some settings of these parameters are better for driving than others. Sometimes it's safer to accelerate slowly instead of always flooring the gas pedal. So if you have a way to measure safety, a machine learning algorithm can automatically search for the best settings for the parameters. In this way the search algorithm *automates* a search that otherwise would occupy a person. So instead of doing the searching themselves, AI researchers create systems that search. And because they constantly program these kinds of searching systems, AI researchers naturally become experts in thinking about search. In short, the interesting fact is that they design search algorithms while at the same time *they* are searching as well—for new AI algorithms.

So the search for AI algorithms can be described as a kind of *meta-search*—a search for things that search. In other words, one type of search is nested within another. While things that are "meta" may seem a little mind-bending, in this instance it isn't as complicated as it sounds. In fact, this sort of "meta-search" happens in real life, too. Imagine if you were trying to pick which puppy to take home from a puppy breeder, and you happened to like curious puppies. You'd be searching for the puppy that most likes to search. Or imagine that your job was to hire someone at a treasure-hunting company for the position of senior treasure hunter. You'd be searching for the best treasure hunter, whose job is to search for treasure. So the whole thing is a "meta-search" for treasure. Being a researcher in AI is similar because AI researchers are searching for the best algorithms—and the algorithms themselves may search for the best settings of parameters.

The meta-search perspective is helpful because it illustrates a *connection* between how search algorithms work and how researchers in AI create algorithms. The idea is that AI researchers' expert understanding of search *also* applies to how the AI community as a whole searches for new algorithms. In other words, how search is programmed in the best algorithms in AI should relate somehow to how researchers search for new algorithms. Because whether you're searching for algorithms or for parameters, you're still *searching*. But it turns out that this meta-level of AI research is rarely discussed. That is, not many people talk about the connection between the AI community's search and the insights gained from searching algorithms. While many papers in AI analyze what makes search work on the algorithm level, little is said of the AI community's *meta-search* for the algorithms themselves. But similar principles must apply there as well. After all, search is still search on whatever level.

You'd think that experts on writing world-class search algorithms would also be skilled at guiding a search themselves. So an interesting question is whether the search experts in the AI community avoid chasing the false compass of ambitious objectives—or whether even the experts are drawn to the myth of the objective like everyone else.

*   *   *

To explore whether deception is a real problem in the AI community, we can begin by looking at how the community actually conducts the search for AI algorithms. As we've discussed throughout this book, the key idea behind search is to follow a *gradient*: A bread-crumb trail of some kind, a path of increasing intensity. In objective-driven search, the gradient is moving from bad to good on some performance measure. In novelty search, it's the gradient of novelty. So what gradients do AI researchers follow when searching for new algorithms?

Doing AI research often means first *deciding* which algorithms are the most promising, and then *improving* or extending them in some way. The hope is that this process will lead to newer and even better algorithms. But to decide which AI algorithms are the most promising, what criteria are best for grading them? Choosing which algorithms to further explore should be based on how they behave or perform. So the danger here is that if the information guiding the community is just a simple objective, then it could lead to deception: An algorithm might appear promising based on a performance test but it might not lead to anything better or more interesting. Of course, it's true that ranking algorithms by how they perform on a simple test might make deciding easier. But because of deception it's unlikely that focusing only on algorithms that do the best will lead to anything revolutionary.

We can think of the gradients followed by AI researchers as the information they use to decide which algorithms are the best. A technical term for a rule of thumb that guides search is a *heuristic*. While no one can be *sure* which heuristics will work the best for getting to high-level AI, the AI community has settled upon two in particular. The first, which we'll call the *experimentalist heuristic*, follows the rule of thumb that an algorithm's promise is given by how well it performs. In other words, an algorithm worth exploring further performs *better* than existing algorithms in *benchmark* tasks. Benchmark tasks in AI work like benchmarks in other areas. We benchmark computers for their processing speed, athletes for how fast they can run, and cars for how many miles they can travel per gallon of gas. When scientists benchmark AI, the idea is that a smarter algorithm should solve a problem faster than a weaker algorithm. Besides the experimentalist heuristic, the second main gradient in AI research is the *theoretical heuristic*. This heuristic suggests that algorithms are better if they can be *proven* to have desirable properties. This approach is similar to the idea behind guarantees sold with car parts. Mathematical proofs about algorithms can show that they will have reliable and predictable performance.

Importantly, these two heuristics hold a profound sway over the field. Even if you don't like them or have your own philosophy, you won't publish many of your ideas without respecting them. In the field of AI, the gatekeepers who decide what is published wield these heuristics with an iron fist. If an algorithm *doesn't* improve performance or *doesn't* come with guarantees, it will be hard for it to pass the gatekeepers—and so it will probably never become known to the AI community as a whole. As a result, the two main heuristics of the AI community have a huge impact on which ideas are explored.

But this situation doesn't only arise in the field of AI. Every research community depends on heuristics of some kind to filter ideas—they just might not be the same measures that are used in AI. The information that reviewers consider to decide whether to publish a new idea *must* be a rule of thumb, because there's no way to know for sure where a new idea will lead down the road. So over time, it's natural for the culture of each scientific discipline to converge on some general rules of thumb for filtering ideas. Even though the particular heuristics will vary from field to field, there's a lot to learn even from the *particular* rules of thumb that guide AI research. This kind of case study can illuminate the *general* problems with the rules of thumb used to judge new scientific research. And if the AI community—whose researchers are experts in search—still can't escape these problems, then other fields may also be susceptible to similar mistakes.

Perhaps it isn't obvious that there are problems with the way the AI community conducts research at all. The experimentalist and theoretical heuristics may sound perfectly logical. For one thing, some ideas really are bad and presenting those bad ideas to the community would just waste everyone's valuable time. Why would we want to learn about an algorithm that performs *worse*, or that doesn't come with promises about what it's good for? Because even if the algorithm's performance could be improved, or something could eventually be proven about it, wouldn't it be better just to let its authors fix the algorithm and then submit the *fixed* algorithm instead? That way, there'd be no risk of wasting so many people's time on such a questionable algorithm. These arguments are so obvious that they're almost never actually made. Who would need to argue that ideas that perform worse should receive less attention? It's common knowledge. But it's also "common knowledge" that objectives are a good way to guide search. We need to be careful about common knowledge.

First, let's look at the experimentalist heuristic. It considers a new algorithm as promising only if it outperforms the algorithms that are the current favorites. And it turns out that the most common complaint reviewers make about a new algorithm in AI is that its performance is unimpressive or unclear. Many reviewers believe that to showcase an algorithm's capabilities, it should always be compared to many of the best algorithms on many challenging problems. So reviewers might justify rejecting a paper with something like, "The authors should have also compared their new method to method *OldReliable*," or, "The authors should also run an experiment in the *UnrelatedButTough* problem to be sure that this new idea is actually an important step forward." And many of us who work in AI have had these very thoughts ourselves!

But this custom can be dangerous. As J.N. Hooker writes: "Most experimental studies of heuristic algorithms resemble track meets more than scientific endeavors [126]." Recall that AI is a search for algorithms that search—a meta-search. So with this meta-search in mind it's probably not a good idea always to reject new ideas just because their performance is unimpressive. Recall that *performance* is exactly the heuristic against which novelty search compared favorably in Chap. 5. There's no reason to suspect that the *same* heuristic, but used one level up (to guide the AI community as a whole instead of a search algorithm), will avoid the problems plaguing objective-driven search. When performance is the rule of thumb that filters which algorithms are shown to the larger community, all other kinds of stepping stones are rejected and ignored. It would be one thing if criticisms about performance were just criticisms—and not a standard reason for rejection. But because performance is so widely accepted as a filter for new ideas, it becomes a classic deceptive objective function.

For example, imagine that for many years the most popular way to train robots to perform difficult tasks was the algorithm called *OldReliable*. Then one day a group of scientists invents a new algorithm called *Weird*. While *Weird* teaches robots similar skills as *OldReliable*, the newer algorithm is very novel. So the journal reviewers trying to decide whether *Weird* should be published haven't seen anything like it before. To make matters more complicated, in the study that they submit for publication, the authors' new algorithm *Weird* performs 5 % *worse* than *OldReliable* on a standard benchmark (like teaching a robot how to walk). These kinds of comparisons are common: Perhaps algorithm *Weird* takes 5 % longer to learn how to walk or it learns a walking gait that is 5 % less stable.

Because it performs worse, the experimentalist heuristic supports rejecting *Weird*. It's very unusual that new research papers in AI advertise a new algorithm by reporting that it performs *worse*. Most authors wouldn't even bother submitting that kind of study. They're well aware that the experimentalist heuristic is a powerful filter for research in AI. So if a new algorithm doesn't perform better than its competitors on one benchmark, its inventors often will try to improve its performance or find a more favorable benchmark.

But suppose that the authors are stubborn and submit the work where *Weird* performs 5 % worse anyway. Although the reviewers are likely to do so, does rejecting *Weird* really make sense? It's a completely *new* research direction, full of new ideas. The key problem is that by rejecting *Weird*, no one will hear about it. What's worse is that there will be no one to explore all the stepping stones that are opened up by *Weird* that extend *beyond* it. So the experimentalist heuristic is short-sighted: It judges *Weird* for its *present* value rather than the value of the *future* it opens up for AI research. Because its potential isn't appreciated, *Weird* and all the algorithms beyond it are swept away to the academic dustbin. These kinds of sweeping rejections *prune away* a large part of the search space, the space of all AI algorithms. Those pruned-away parts of the space then won't ever be explored because they're only reachable from algorithms that aren't great performers.

If you agree with much of what we've said in this book, then you might think that because *Weird* is so innovative it should be accepted no matter how it compares to *OldReliable*. But there's a bigger question here. Why was *Weird* compared to *OldReliable* at all? The comparison only distracts us from *what makes Weird interesting* in the first place—which may be a better place to focus. But to pass the experimentalist heuristic's filter researchers must make these distracting comparisons.

To put the problem in a slightly more farcical light, imagine that a windup toy soldier is pitted against a humanoid robot in a footrace. While the humanoid tries its best to keep up, the windup toy is just too fast and wins by a large margin. But what exactly does this footrace mean for humanoid robot research? Should we forget about walking robots entirely until they can beat windup toys? Of course, the race result really suggests *nothing* at all, because windup toys and humanoid robots are apples and oranges. And that's the biggest problem with the experimentalist heuristic: The *reason* we're interested in humanoid robots has nothing to do with footraces against windup toys. Likewise, the reason we're interested in the algorithm *Weird* might have nothing to do with how it compares to algorithm *OldReliable*. It may be inconvenient, but what makes for a good stepping stone is more slippery than we'd like. There doesn't seem to be a simple formula for it. An objective heuristic like measuring a new algorithm on a battery of benchmark tasks may *feel* comforting—it's backed by a clear principle and makes it easy to mindlessly judge new algorithms. But benchmarks do little to illuminate *why* one research direction is more or less *interesting* than another.

The problem with relying too much on experimental results and comparisons is that they can be highly deceptive. Method *Weird* may very well be the seed of a new AI revolution, but it's lost on a 5 % technicality. And the race between the windup toy and the humanoid is silly because we learn nothing from comparing them— humanoid robots are interesting no matter how badly they compare to toys in a race. All this just goes to show that sometimes the experimentalist heuristic can act like a Chinese finger trap. It's always advising us to *pull harder* when what we might really need to do, even though it scores worse on the objective function at first, is to *push*.

The root of the problem is that the experimentalist heuristic is driven by an objective, which as usual stifles exploration. In this case, the unstated objective is *perfect performance*, and all new algorithms are measured against it. If they seem to improve performance even a little bit, algorithms are rewarded with exposure and adoption. But if they fail to inch performance forward, they're dismissed and ignored. The result is that the *field* of AI is drawn into a classic objective-driven search—which is fueled by the assumption that objective-driven searches work well. But there's an interesting irony here: The experimentalist heuristic is driven by such a simple objective that few AI researchers would actually employ an *algorithm* based on such a naïve heuristic today.

While *algorithms* that search have become more sophisticated to deal with some level of deception, these insights aren't being applied to how AI researchers them- selves behave in their search as a community. So even as the simple experimentalist heuristic hides in plain sight, the field is driven faithfully by it. Somehow it avoids the questioning it deserves. In fact, this strange disconnect shows how attractive naïve objective-driven efforts are: Even a community of experts in the theory of search still finds itself swearing by them.

There's another way to see the problem with the experimentalist heuristic—by thinking about the *search space*. In this case the search space contains all possible AI algorithms. So both algorithm *OldReliable* and algorithm *Weird* are single *points* in this larger space. Recall the great room of all possible things from Chap. 1. In AI, the room is filled with algorithms, teeming from wall to wall and ceiling to ceiling. And remember that there's some logic to the layout of this great room of algorithms. Along one wall you might find a simple algorithm to sort a list of numbers in increasing order, and right next to it you might find a slight tweak of the same algorithm that sorts the list in decreasing order instead.

Because it contains all algorithms, somewhere in this vast space is the familiar algorithm *OldReliable*, surrounded by similar algorithms nearby. And far away in another corner is the newcomer, algorithm *Weird*. What this scenario shows is that the experimentalist heuristic often asks us to compare the performance of two *distant* points in a giant search space. It's like the footrace between robots and wind-up toys. And in most searches it doesn't make sense to be guided by this kind of strange comparison—it doesn't help us decide where to look next in the great room. Does Van Gogh's Starry Night suggest that we shouldn't care about Michelangelo's David? Does a train suggest we should stop inventing better bicycles? Oranges aren't a reason to stop breeding apples, even if you like oranges better. Of course some people will continue breeding better apples and some will breed better oranges, and it's in all our interests that *both* directions are explored.

On the other hand, we don't mean to suggest that no one should ever investigate whether *OldReliable* outperforms *Weird*. The outcome of the comparison might still provide insight to some—even though it can cause deception when *guiding* the search for algorithms. To understand why, it's important to consider the difference between AI *researchers* and AI *practitioners*. While researchers blaze trails toward future innovation, the practitioner wants to solve real-world problems right now. Instead of trying to make new algorithms, a practitioner looks at the algorithms available *today* and then decides which to apply to a present problem. It's like the difference between inventing new experimental types of cars and choosing which car to buy from a dealership. The practitioner is more an AI customer than an AI inventor. The important distinction is that the practitioner doesn't participate in the search for *new* algorithms. For her a solution is needed today, and the best algorithm available will just have to do. So you can see how a comparison between *OldReliable* and *Weird* might help a practitioner make an informed choice today. If *OldReliable* is 5 % better in a benchmark that resembles the problem the practitioner is trying to solve, then she should probably use *OldReliable* over *Weird*. But we shouldn't allow this distinction to confuse us—what's best for the practitioner needn't be connected to what's best for the researcher. The automobile researcher shouldn't quit her job if she finds out that a Ford Taurus gets better gas mileage than her levitating jet-car prototype.

Recall that we want to understand how *researchers* judge *new* algorithms. More importantly, we'd like to understand how those judgments decide which stepping stones are explored to create even newer algorithms. So what's interesting for the practitioner—who is frozen at one moment in time—isn't the right compass for an innovator looking towards the future. Perhaps the confusion between these two roles (practitioner and researcher) might help explain how the experimentalist heuristic came to dominate AI (and how similar rules of thumb became popular in many other fields). Judging by performance is a good idea for practitioners but is shaky at best for researchers—because of deception.

But as we mentioned earlier, the experimentalist heuristic isn't alone. The other main rule of thumb in the search for AI algorithms is the *theoretical heuristic*. Its core idea is that algorithms with more proven *guarantees* are the most promising for further exploration. In fact, some researchers view the theoretical heuristic as a better choice than the experimentalist heuristic because it offers indisputable guarantees. The experimentalist heuristic doesn't *prove* when *OldReliable* will outperform *Weird* or how much the results depend on particular settings—it just shows that in *some* cases *OldReliable* is better. The nice thing about theoretical results (those that rely on mathematical proofs) is that they always include the conditions in which the theory holds. So as long as those conditions are met, then you know to some extent what to expect from the algorithm. But even though guarantees may seem like a solid foundation, it turns out that the theoretical heuristic is flawed as well. Perhaps surprisingly, it suffers from the same defect as the experimentalist heuristic when it's used to guide the search for AI algorithms.

But before we pinpoint that defect, there's something strange about the phrase "theoretical heuristic"—the words "theoretical" and "heuristic" seem like they're opposites. As researchers in AI are well aware, *heuristics* are rules of thumb. What sense is there in a "guaranteed rule of thumb?" While heuristics may work more often than not, they don't often guarantee progress. But mathematical theorems, on the other hand, *do* offer guarantees—so they can't be questioned in the same way. One might ask whether a particular heuristic will really work in a given problem, but it doesn't make sense to question whether a particular theorem will still be true. Once a theorem is proven to be true, it will always be true. This reliability is one reason that theorems are so appealing to the AI community: If we can *prove* that a particular algorithm will succeed under certain conditions, the resulting guarantee can't be revoked. So in the phrase "theoretical heuristic," the uncertainty of heuristics may seem to clash with the invincibility of theorems.

But the words do fit together here because they're acting on two different levels of the meta-search for AI algorithms. The word "theoretical" applies to an individual algorithm by asking whether there are good guarantees for that algorithm. In contrast, the word "heuristic" applies to the search *through* AI algorithms, suggesting that algorithms with lots of proven guarantees may often make good stepping stones. Once again, things that are meta can sometimes be hard to grasp, but there's really nothing too complicated going on here. It's just that theorems (the theoretical part) are being used as a rule of thumb (the heuristic part) for what makes a good algorithm. What's important is that the research community shouldn't focus only on particular theorems about AI algorithms. It's not even best to focus on particular AI algorithms themselves. No, overall we should be focusing on *exploring* the space of all AI algorithms and uncovering promising stepping stones. So what we're looking at here is *how theorems are used to guide exploration through the space of AI algorithms.* The amount of good theoretical results about an algorithm *serves* as a heuristic inside the higher-level search for algorithms conducted by the AI community. All other things being equal, the community typically prefers algorithms with *more* theoretical guarantees.

For example, suppose that a theoretician proves a new theorem about the algorithm *OldReliable*. The new theorem guarantees that algorithm *OldReliable* will produce an acceptable result reasonably quickly. This sort of theorem is a goal of AI theorists because it promises *practitioners* that the algorithm will produce a reasonable result. So it makes sense for a practitioner to choose an algorithm with many theorems backing it instead of one with no theorems. But a theorem about one particular algorithm doesn't promise anything about *future algorithms* that may be invented by *researchers* searching the space of algorithms. In other words, this new theorem is *about* algorithm *OldReliable*—it doesn't promise anything about later algorithms that are stepping stones *beyond* algorithm *OldReliable*. The theorem doesn't guarantee that *they* will have the same guarantee, and it also doesn't guarantee that they will *ever* be any better than algorithm *OldReliable* even if they did.

While a theorist might respond that the benefit of the theorem *is* that any future algorithm that honors the same assumptions will inherit the same guarantees, this fact is not necessarily good news for encouraging the exploration of new ideas. It means that the community becomes restricted only to those algorithms that honor the same growing set of assumptions, blinding the meta-search to every path forward that breaks the assumptions. In the end, the effect is less exploration—the objective paradox takes it hold.

The problem is that the theorem isn't a theorem about what the *community* should do next. The theorem is about one algorithm—one point in the huge search space of all possible algorithms. For all we know, a tiny change to an algorithm that *isn't* proven to perform well could create an algorithm that performs even better than algorithm *OldReliable* does. A proof for one algorithm doesn't say anything about other algorithms that may come up in the future. So to believe that algorithm *OldReliable* is a promising stepping stone *because of its theorem* only makes sense if there's something about this particular theorem that *suggests* the algorithm may lead to other promising algorithms. Whenever you choose which rule of thumb to rely on—whether it's the experimentalist or the theoretical heuristic—don't forget that you're still just relying on your intuition. Whether you like performance or guarantees, they're both intuitions about what clues hint that an algorithm is a promising stepping stone. The main issue with the theoretical heuristic is that theorems speak about particular algorithms. So the amount of theorems for an algorithm can be no more than a rule of thumb for its promise as a stepping stone to new algorithms. In the end, there's nothing to reassure us that the theoretical heuristic is any more reliable than the experimentalist heuristic.

Another problem is that the theoretical heuristic assumes that there's a particular *structure* to the search space of algorithms. The assumption is that the more promising theorems you have about an algorithm, the closer you are to the objectives of AI. But this belief is just an assumption. Within the vast search space that AI researchers are looking through, it's not clear that theorems about algorithms will indicate that the loftiest objectives of AI are nearby. Even if *OldReliable* has a theorem that guarantees performance while algorithm *Weird* doesn't, it doesn't mean that *Weird* isn't important. It may be highly novel and raise several interesting new issues—even if it performs poorly *and* lacks a guarantee. If algorithm *Weird* does have potential, then why ignore it? Putting too much faith in the theoretical heuristic just delays (or prevents) exploring the ideas that are raised by *Weird*.

But some might say that we should simply *wait* for a proven performance theorem for algorithm *Weird*. That way we won't waste our time on unproven algorithms. We might be waiting several years though, because it's hard to prove an ambitious theoretical result. It's never clear which guarantees can be proven either. So if *Weird* could lead to a new algorithm *Weirder*, which is interesting for reasons having nothing to do with *Weird*'s guarantees, then the effect of waiting is just that it takes us several years longer to visit *Weirder*. The AI community is held back as a result. Of course, AI practitioners may appreciate the guarantee for *Weird*, but once again the practitioners don't participate in the search for AI. While theorems are interesting, it's not clear that performance guarantees (or any other guarantees) are the right kind of information to guide search on their own—especially through a space as vast and complicated as the great room of all AI algorithms.

We're left with the uncomfortable fact (although it's familiar by now) that it isn't clear that *any* rule of thumb can be a reliable guide to the objectives of AI. Of course, that doesn't mean that all experiments or all theorems are worthless. At the same time, they're just one grain of evidence in a sea of possible clues. While higher performance or a surprising new theorem may be *impressive* achievements, *being impressed* also isn't a reliable guide for reaching particular objectives in a search. Windup toys may waddle impressively fast, but it's not likely that they'll end up being the bridge to a revolution in robotics.

At its heart, the theoretical heuristic relies on the belief that securing guarantees leads to securing even *more* and better guarantees. So it defines an objective gradient through the space of AI algorithms. If we believe in this gradient, and if it really works and doesn't lead to deception, then eventually it will lead to guarantees so powerful that AI is achieved. But does it really makes sense that a set of stepping stones of increasing guarantees could lay a convenient path to human-level AI? In fact, some truths are *unprovable* [127]. For all we know, the most powerful AI algorithms provide few guarantees at all.

After all, natural evolution *did* discover human intelligence, but it never proved a single theorem during its entire epic run. Even without theorems, evolution collected stepping stone after stepping stone, eventually building a bridge to intelligence. This story doesn't prove that the theoretical heuristic is a bad gradient to follow, but it certainly shows that we don't *need* theorems to go far. And it's at least thought-provoking that the most powerful search ever to produce intelligence had no use for theorems along the way. The deeper point is that the theoretical heuristic creates a kind of objective-driven search through the space of AI algorithms—and we know now from experience how those kinds of searches generally perform in complex spaces.

The experimentalist heuristic and theoretical heuristic aren't just rules of thumb. They aren't just tools used by scientists toiling alone in the dark of night. No, these are the iron yardsticks wielded by gatekeepers of the AI community. Their measurements decide what ideas are good enough to share. Whether you like these yardsticks or not, whether you want to use them or not, whether or not AI *actually does* lie along their paths, you'll still fight to publish any of your ideas without satisfying them in some way. If your algorithm performs worse than the status quo, then your reasoning for why anyone should see it will be tortured. But if you don't compare your approach to others, then most will dismiss it as unproven. And if you don't have theorems to back up your new idea, you'll be hard-pressed to convince AI theorists that anyone should care. And the fallout is severe: The iron yardstick forces the community onto the narrow sets of stepping stones that pass these heuristics. Little else will be considered.

But as we've seen, these heuristics actually stand in the way of discovery and progress, because they only make sense when lit by the broken myth of the objective. As usual, the natural question is whether there's a promising non-objective replacement for the objective-driven status quo? Is there a way to guide AI research that more resembles the treasure hunter, one that respects the intrinsic promise of stepping stones over deceptive mechanical heuristics?

To begin to answer this question, let's start from square one and rethink what we should be seeking in the first place. What *really* makes a "good" AI algorithm? The community is so focused on performance that it misses the forest for the trees: *A good algorithm isn't one that performs better, but one that leads us to think of other algorithms.* The objectives of AI are so far off across the mist-cloaked lake that we shouldn't worry so much about the ruler of performance. Current algorithms are so distant from human-level intelligence that we're echoing the thought experiment from Chap. 4 in which bacteria are given IQ tests. We shouldn't be concerned with whether *Weird* is better than *OldReliable*. Instead, we should ask whether *Weird* leads to a new algorithm *Weirder*, which extends *Weird* along *any* interesting dimension (not just performance). For example, *Weirder* might create brain-like structures that *look* more like real-world brains than *Weird*, even if they perform worse. Should we drop a new idea for worse performance alone? The community is engaged in a *search* after all, and a search's function is to *find things*. The experimentalist and theoretical heuristics are about finding *fewer* things because they prune out many interesting algorithms.

The journals of AI are overflowing with performance improvements. And every AI researcher attending a conference can look forward to talks reporting 2 % improvements through complicated tricks. Maybe the solution is that conferences should accept even fewer papers because 2 % is "too small" to be worthwhile. Maybe standards need to rise! But that's the wrong message. The problem isn't that the improvements are too tiny. The problem is that no one follows up on most of these algorithms—there's no exciting insight in squeezing out the last bit of performance through hairsplitting details. The problem is that performance-squeezing algorithms just *aren't good stepping stones*. The algorithms that are remembered, just as with all human inventions, are those that lay the foundation for future trailblazers. They lead to creating new algorithms and perhaps even entirely new fields. At that point, who cares about how they initially performed in a comparison against *OldReliable*?

Another effect of the obsession with increased performance is that it pits researchers against each other. Science isn't a track meet. This competition often distracts from the real purpose of the AI community: to work together to explore the space of AI algorithms. But here's what often happens instead—one researcher will show that his algorithm performs better than the current leader. The usual response is for another researcher then to knock the new leader off its pedestal. For example, if algorithm *Weird* performs better than the standby *OldReliable* in a popular benchmark, a heroic researcher swoops down to save the day. This hero will show that actually another algorithm *Diversion* beats *Weird* in a *different* benchmark—which brings *Weird* back to Earth—so it's not the best after all. And while it may seem good to set the facts straight, this intense competition over benchmarks distracts us from anything but performance. If algorithm *Weird* is genuinely radical and a stepping stone to new frontiers, the story of its battle with *Diversion* is only a sideshow. The real blockbuster will be *Weird*'s sequel: *Weirder*. As always, the stepping stones are the true stars.

*　　　　*　　　　*

From this case study of AI, we've seen how objective heuristics can restrict exploration in a scientific community. But even if we accept these flaws, how can a community flourish without *any* compass? Can the AI community run some kind of "novelty search" over AI algorithms? Yes, something like that is possible, but it would require an overhaul to put into practice.

Think back to Picbreeder. There are no *rules* in that community. There's no panel of experts that decide whether a user's picture is really worth sharing. There aren't any rigid yardsticks that objectively show which picture is "best." There's no rule that each published image must be compared with rival images to show that it's better, or that the author of an image must *prove* its value to the community. There aren't any of these checks and balances in Picbreeder. Even so, the Picbreeder community has no problem finding the unfindable: complex mathematical expressions (which are the "DNA" in Picbreeder) that describe remarkably meaningful images—the needles in the haystack of all possible images. No one could find the Picbreeder *Skull* on his or her own. It took a community, a community *without* gatekeepers driven by objectives.

"False analogy," you might say. Selecting interesting images doesn't require expertise or experience. The field of AI requires both. We can't simply allow anyone with any crazy idea to publish their algorithms (if they even deserve to be called that) to the community. The experimentalist and theoretical heuristics protect us against a flood of craziness. At least we know that if authors prove some level of performance then their algorithm isn't a fraud.

While this argument sounds reasonable, it ignores a key fact about AI researchers (and all other humans): We have brains. Isn't it strange to say that we must *protect* ourselves from potential cranks by following rigid objective rules? Is it really true that without objective heuristics we couldn't identify nonsense when we see it? Of course expertise is important in the scientific community. Just as you want professional engineers to design the airplane that flies you overseas, experts—and not randomly chosen people—should be making decisions on what other experts might want to see. But to leave those decisions to objective heuristics doesn't *honor* the role of experts, but instead *denies* it. It's even perhaps insulting to imply that experts are dangerously gullible, and that the community is saved from crazy ideas *only because* of those heuristics. If the heuristics are necessary, then we must not trust the experts to use their brains. Then what kind of experts can they really be anyway?

It's not that the experts can't be trusted. The real issue is that the experimentalist and theoretical heuristics, as with many objective measures in society, become excuses *not* to use our brains, even for the experts. Reviewers can simply dismiss an algorithm that they don't like if it performs worse than an algorithm that they do like. And if it performs better, they can simply demand that its creators compare it to many more algorithms before finally giving it the green light. When the experts don't use their brains, the discussion is shifted away from the *substance* of what makes an algorithm interesting. It's shifted instead to a simple objective yardstick in the search space, an endless race against the latest wind-up toys. It just happens to be easier to evaluate ideas with simple rules of thumb. To examine ideas deeply, and to consider what they may make possible in the future is tough intellectual work, especially with unfamiliar ideas.

So let's try one final thought experiment for the book: Let's pretend that there's a very unusual journal in the field of AI called the *Journal of AI Discovery* (or JAID for short). But unlike any other journal in the field of AI, *reviewers* for the journal are not allowed to refer to the *results* of the experiments in their reviews. The *authors* submitting their studies to JAID may include theoretical and experimental results as usual, but the *reviewers* can't base their reviews on those results. So the reviewers are barred from criticizing a new algorithm because its performance is worse than another. They also can't claim that more comparisons and more benchmarks are needed (the answer doesn't matter for JAID). They can't complain that theoretical guarantees aren't provided. They can't criticize that theoretical results are not good enough. But beyond these rules, the reviewers can argue however they like for whether the *idea* should be published or not. And importantly, these reviewers aren't just random people, but are chosen from the cream of the crop of AI researchers.

The question is: Are the articles published in JAID worse than those published in the most distinguished journals in the field? Or are they far better? Would you read JAID if you were an AI researcher, knowing that its reviewers can't criticize (or reward) performance measures or demand guarantees?

What JAID does is *challenge* its reviewers to engage with the *substance* of an article. They're freed from the experimentalist and theoretical heuristics of AI. This means that they're forced to *think* about the core idea and decide whether it's *interesting*. If it's interesting then it might be a good stepping stone. These reviewers are the greatest minds of the field—they should be able to deeply consider how the idea might change the field. So instead of the traditional heuristics, their minds have to digest the meat of the idea. There aren't any clear rules for quick dismissal or acceptance. It will require real and difficult consideration.

Instead of speculating about how much JAID would impact the field, let's explore an interesting paradox that it raises: If JAID proves to be worse than the best traditional journals of AI, then what does that say about the "experts" performing its reviews? But if JAID proves better, then what does that say about the heuristics guiding the field? Either way, something's wrong. If we can only think objectively, then we aren't thinking much at all. There's no substitute for using our minds because science can't provide a fixed *method* to discover the next great idea. The greatest ideas are unlike those that came before them. Every stepping stone has a unique story of discovery. And every human being who found one has a story too.

A real expert in any field can think with an open mind and doesn't need a rigid heuristic to make a decision. It's difficult to consider an entirely new idea in all its detail. It takes dedicated effort and time. There may be many subtle points that are easy to overlook and new concepts that may be hard to digest. It's harder to give an idea a fair shake than to judge results quickly on simple rules of thumb— which can also help to maintain the status quo. If a new idea seems strange, you can simply demand more guarantees or better performance results—instead of bothering to understand it. And it very well might seem reasonable to make such demands, because you're just protecting the community from algorithms that fail to measure up.

But as John Stewart Mill knew even in 1846, it's wrong to assume that the stepping stones *will resemble* where they ultimately lead [128]. Good performance isn't a stepping stone to revolutionary performance. Guarantees aren't stepping stones to revelations. In case it's hard to think of alternatives to arguing about performance or guarantees, there are in fact many other important clues we can consider: *inspiration, elegance, potential to provoke further creativity, thought-provoking construction, challenge to the status quo, novelty, analogy to nature, beauty, simplicity, and imagination*. All of these are possible for a new algorithm or any other kind of new idea. While they may lack objectivity, perhaps that is *exactly* what can liberate the field of AI, and many other fields at that. Anyone can say that performance should improve, but who has the courage to see the *beauty* of an idea? We could use a few more brave experts like that.

Bibliography

1. D. Godse and A. P. Godse, *Computer Organisation and Architecture*. Technical Publications Pune, 2009.
2. Wikipedia, "Instructions per second," 2011.
3. S. Okamura, *History of electron tubes*. IOS Press, 1994.
4. J. Levy, *Really useful: the origins of everyday things*. Firefly Books Ltd, 2002.
5. A. Hyman, *Charles Babbage: Pioneer of the computer*. Princeton University Press, 1985.
6. T. E. Larson, *History of rock and roll*. Kendall Hunt Publishing Company, 2004.
7. R. Bolles, *What color is your parachute? A practical manual for job hunters and career changers*. Ten Speed Press, Berkeley, 1984.
8. "Career key test." http://www.careerkey.org, 2012.
9. D. Campbell, "Campbell interest and skill survey (CISS)," *Upper Saddle River, NJ: Pearson Assessments, Pearson Education, Last accessed December*, vol. 28, 1970.
10. I. Myers and P. Myers, *Gifts differing: Understanding personality type*. Nicholas Brealey Boston, 1980.
11. D. Keirsey, *Please understand me*. Prometheus Nemesis, 2007.
12. R. Wiseman, *The luck factor: The scientific study of the lucky mind*. Gardners Books, 2004.
13. J. Hunter, *Johnny Depp: movie top ten*. Creation Pub Group, 1999.
14. "John Grisham: The official site." http://www.jgrisham.com/bio, 2012.
15. C. Kirk, *JK Rowling: a biography*. Greenwood Publishing Group, 2003.
16. J. Rubin, *Haruki Murakami and the music of words*. Vintage Books, 2005.
17. T. Hiney, *Raymond Chandler: a biography*. Grove Press, 1999.
18. R. Martin and A. Bailey, *First Philosophy: Fundamental Problems and Readings in Philosophy*, vol. 3. Broadview Press, 2011.
19. P. Brown, S. Gaines, and A. DeCurtis, *The love you make: an insider's story of the Beatles*. Penguin, 2002.
20. P. Norman, *Sir Elton*. Pan, 2011.
21. H. Sanders, *Life as I Have Known it Has Been Finger Lickin'Good*. Creation House, 1974.
22. D. Betsworth and J. Hansen, "The categorization of serendipitous career development events," *Journal of Career Assessment*, vol. 4, no. 1, pp. 91–98, 1996.
23. J. Bright, R. Pryor, S. Wilkenfeld, and J. Earl, "The role of social context and serendipitous events in career decision making," *International Journal for Educational and Vocational Guidance*, vol. 5, no. 1, pp. 19–36, 2005.
24. D. Lawrence, *The complete poems of DH Lawrence*. Wordsworth Editions Ltd, 1994.
25. P. Eastwick, E. Finkel, and A. Eagly, "When and why do ideal partner preferences affect the process of initiating and maintaining romantic relationships?," 2011.

© Springer International Publishing Switzerland 2015

K.O. Stanley, J. Lehman, *Why Greatness Cannot Be Planned*,

DOI 10.1007/978-3-319-15524-1

26. S. Otfinoski, *Calvin Coolidge*. Marshall Cavendish Children's Books, 2008.

27. N. Sawaya, *The Art of The Brick*. 2008.

28. "Joseph herscher's homepage." http://www.joesephherscher.com, 2012.

29. K. Ginsburg *et al.*, "The importance of play in promoting healthy child development and maintaining strong parent-child bonds," *AAP Policy*, vol. 119, no. 1, p. 182, 2007.

30. A. Rosenfeld, N. Wise, and R. Coles, *The over-scheduled child: Avoiding the hyper-parenting trap*. Griffin, 2001.

31. P. Bahn and J. Vertut, *Journey through the ice age*. University of California Press, 1997.

32. F. Levy, *15 Minutes of Fame: Becoming a Star in the YouTube Revolution*. Penguin, 2008.

33. J. Livingston, *Founders at Work: Stories of Startups' Early Days*. Springer, 2008.

34. D. Sheff, *Game over: how Nintendo zapped an American industry, captured your dollars, and enslaved your children*. Random House Inc., 1993.

35. R. Dawkins, *The Blind Watchmaker: Why the evidence of evolution reveals a universe without design*. W.W. Norton and Company, 1986.

36. H. Takagi, "Interactive evolutionary computation: Fusion of the capabilities of ec optimization and human evaluation," *Proceedings of the IEEE*, vol. 89, no. 9, pp. 1275–1296, 2001.

37. B. Woolley and K. Stanley, "On the deleterious effects of a priori objectives on evolution and representation," in *Proceedings of the 13th annual conference on Genetic and evolutionary computation*, pp. 957–964, ACM, 2011.

38. P. E. Ceruzzi, *A history of modern computing*. MIT press, 2003.

39. H. Curtis and A. Filippone, *Aerospace engineering desk reference*. Butterworth-Heinemann, 2009.

40. J. Mokyr and F. Scherer, *Twenty five centuries of technological change: an historical survey*, vol. 35. Routledge, 1990.

41. R. Wiseman, *Quirkology: The curious science of everyday lives*. Pan, 2008.

42. A. N. Whitehead, *Adventures of Ideas*. The Free Press, 1967.

43. W. Stace, "Interestingness," *Philosophy*, vol. 19, no. 74, pp. 233–241, 1944.

44. W. Stukeley, *Memoirs of Sir Isaac Newton's life*. 1752.

45. R. Roberts, *Serendipity: Accidental discoveries in science*. Wiley, 1989.

46. W. Whewell, *The Philosophy of the inductive sciences: founded upon their history*, vol. 2. 1840.

47. L. Pasteur, 1854.

48. S. J. Gould, *Full House: The Spread of Excellence from Plato to Darwin*. Harmony Books, 1996.

49. J. Lehman and K. O. Stanley, "Abandoning objectives: Evolution through the search for novelty alone," *Evolutionary Computation*, vol. 19, no. 2, pp. 189–223, 2011.

50. J.-B. Mouret, "Novelty-based multiobjectivization," in *Proceedings of the Workshop on Exploring New Horizons in Evolutionary Design of Robots, 2009 IEEE/RSJ International Conference on Intelligent Robots and Systems*, 2009.

51. J. Doucette and M. Heywood, "Novelty-Based Fitness: An Evaluation under the Santa Fe Trail," *Genetic Programming*, pp. 50–61, 2010.

52. P. Krcah, "Solving deceptive tasks in robot body-brain co-evolution by searching for behavioral novelty," in *ISDA*, pp. 284–289, IEEE, 2010.

53. H. Goldsby and B. Cheng, "Automatically Discovering Properties that Specify the Latent Behavior of UML Models," in *Proceedings of MODELS 2010*, 2010.

54. S. Risi, C. Hughes, and K. Stanley, "Evolving plastic neural networks with novelty search," *Adaptive Behavior*, 2010.

55. J. Lehman and K. O. Stanley, "Novelty search and the problem with objectives," in *Genetic Programming in Theory and Practice IX (GPTP 2011)*, ch. 3, pp. 37–56, Springer, 2011.

56. J. Lehman and K. O. Stanley, "Revising the evolutionary computation abstraction: Minimal criteria novelty search," in *Proceedings of the Genetic and Evolutionary Computation Conference (GECCO-2010)*, ACM, 2010.

57. D. H. Wolpert and W. Macready, "No free lunch theorems for optimization," *IEEE Transactions on Evolutionary Computation*, vol. 1, pp. 67–82, 1997.

58. D. Campbell, "Assessing the impact of planned social change," *Evaluation and Program Planning*, vol. 2, no. 1, pp. 67–90, 1979.
59. L. Darling-Hammond and A. E. Wise, "Beyond standardization: State standards and school improvement," *The Elementary School Journal*, pp. 315–336, 1985.
60. M. A. Barksdale-Ladd and K. F. Thomas, "What's at stake in high-stakes testing teachers and parents speak out," *Journal of Teacher Education*, vol. 51, no. 5, pp. 384–397, 2000.
61. A. L. Amrein and D. C. Berliner, "High-stakes testing and student learning," *Education Policy Analysis Archives*, vol. 10, p. 18, 2002.
62. J. E. Stiglitz, "GDP fetishism," *The Economists' Voice*, vol. 6, no. 8, 2009.
63. C. Schwarz, *Implementation Guide to Natural Church Development*. ChurchSmart Resources, 1996.
64. M. Vann, "Of rats, rice, and race: The great hanoi rat massacre, an episode in French colonial history," *French Colonial History*, vol. 4, no. 1, pp. 191–203, 2003.
65. R. Davenport-Hines, *The pursuit of oblivion: A global history of narcotics*. WW Norton & Company, 2004.
66. B. Bryson, *A short history of nearly everything*. Transworld Digital, 2010.
67. L. Bebchuk and J. Fried, "Executive compensation at Fannie Mae: A case study of perverse incentives, nonperformance pay, and camouflage," *Olin Center for Law, Economics, and Business Discussion Paper*, no. 505, 2005.
68. U. S. D. of Education, "Florida NCLB cornerstone update letter," 2008. To Eric Smith. On objectives of No Child Left Behind Act of 2001.
69. T. DeMarco, *Controlling software projects: management, measurement, and estimates*. Prentice Hall PTR, 1986.
70. T. DeMarco, "Software engineering: An idea whose time has come and gone?," *Software, IEEE*, vol. 26, no. 4, pp. 96–96, 2009.
71. U. S. D. of Education, "Race to the top assessment program guidance and frequently asked questions," 2010.
72. R. Benjamin and M. Clum, "A new field of dreams: The collegiate learning assessment project.," *Peer Review*, vol. 5, no. 4, pp. 26–29, 2003.
73. ACT, *CAAP Guide to Successful General Education Outcomes Assessment*. ACT, 2011.
74. "Common core state standards FAQ." http://www.corestandards.org/resources/frequently-asked-questions. Accessed: 2013-10-10.
75. M. G. Jones, B. D. Jones, B. Hardin, L. Chapman, T. Yarbrough, and M. Davis, "The impact of high-stakes testing on teachers and students in North Carolina," *Phi Delta Kappan*, pp. 199–203, 1999.
76. J. Valijarvi, P. Linnakyla, P. Kupari, P. Reinikainen, and I. Arffman, *The Finnish Success in PISA–And Some Reasons behind It: PISA 2000*. Institute for Educational Research, 2002.
77. A. Pigafetta, *Magellan's voyage around the world*. The AH Clark Company, 1906.
78. L. C. Wroth, *The voyages of Giovanni da Verrazzano, 1524–1528*. Yale University Press, 1970.
79. R. F. Scott, *Journals: Captain Scott's Last Expedition*. Oxford University Press, 2006.
80. I. Fang, *A History of Mass Communication: Six Information Revolutions*. Taylor & Francis US, 1997.
81. "National Science Foundation." http://www.nsf.gov, 2012.
82. "European Science Foundation." http://www.esf.org, 2012.
83. D. Hull, "Darwin and his critics. the reception of Darwin's theory of evolution by the scientific community," *Cambridge: Mass., Harvard University Press xii, 473p.. Geog*, vol. 1, pp. 1809–1882, 1973.
84. T. Kuhn, *The structure of scientific revolutions*. University of Chicago press, 1996.
85. E. A. Feigenbaum and P. McCorduck, *The fifth generation: Artificial intelligence and Japan's computer challenge to the world*. Addison-Wesley (Reading, Mass.), 1983.
86. G. Faure and T. M. Mensing, "The urge to explore," in *Introduction to Planetary Science*, pp. 1–12, Springer, 2007.

87. M. P. Coleman, "War on cancer and the influence of the medical-industrial complex," *Journal of Cancer Policy*, vol. 1, no. 2, 2013.

88. T. Coburn and J. McCain, "Summertime blues: 100 stimulus projects that give taxpayers the blues," 2010.

89. T. Coburn, "The National Science Foundation: Under the microscope. April, 2011," 2011.

90. R. C. Atkinson, "The golden fleece, science education, and US science policy," *Proceedings of the American Philosophical Society*, pp. 407–417, 1999.

91. G. H. Hardy, *A mathematician's apology*. Cambridge University Press, 1992.

92. D. M. Bishop, *Group theory and chemistry*. Dover Publications, 2012.

93. E. Wigner, *Group theory: and its application to the quantum mechanics of atomic spectra*, vol. 5. Academic Press, 1959.

94. S. D. Galbraith, *Mathematics of public key cryptography*. Cambridge University Press, 2012.

95. L. S. Smith, "High quality research act," 2013.

96. H. Hoag, "Canadian research shift makes waves.," *Nature*, vol. 472, no. 7343, p. 269, 2011.

97. N. R. Council, "About NRC press release." http://www.nrc-cnrc.gc.ca/eng/news/releases/2013/nrc_business_backgrounder.html. Accessed: 2013-10-10.

98. P. Feyerabend, *Against method*. Verso Books, 1975.

99. C. Morris, *Tesla Motors: How Elon Musk and Company Made Electric Cars Cool, and Sparked the Next Tech Revolution*. Bluespages, 2014.

100. M. Stokstad, *Art, A Brief History*. Pearson, Prentice Hall, 2000.

101. D. Goldberg and L. Larsson, *Minecraft: The Unlikely Tale of Markus" Notch" Persson and the Game that Changed Everything*. Seven Stories Press, 2013.

102. "Mineception - minecraft in minecraft." http://www.planetminecraft.com/project/mineception---minecraft-in-minecraft/, 2012.

103. C. Schifter and M. Cipollone, "Minecraft as a teaching tool: One case study," in *Society for Information Technology & Teacher Education International Conference*, vol. 2013, pp. 2951–2955, 2013.

104. A. White, *Advertising design and typography*. Allworth Press, 2006.

105. T. Crouch and P. Jakab, *The Wright brothers and the invention of the aerial age*. National Geographic, 2003.

106. M. Ruse, *The evolution wars: A guide to the debates*. Rutgers University Press, 2001.

107. N. Copernicus, *De revolutionibus orbium coelestium*. 1543.

108. F. Wöhler, "Ueber künstliche bildung des harnstoffs," *Annalen der Physik*, vol. 88, no. 2, pp. 253–256, 1828.

109. C. Darwin, *On the Origin of Species by Means of Natural Selection or the Preservation of Favored Races in the Struggle for Life*. London: Murray, 1859.

110. E. Daniel, C. Mee, and M. Clark, *Magnetic recording: the first 100 years*. Wiley-IEEE Press, 1999.

111. J. Ulin, *The business of media distribution: monetizing film, TV, and video content*. Focal Press, 2009.

112. A. Grant and J. Meadows, *Communication technology update and fundamentals*. Focal Press, 2010.

113. D. Reagan and R. Waide, *The food web of a tropical rain forest*. University of Chicago Press, 1996.

114. R. Lande, "Natural selection and random genetic drift in phenotypic evolution," *Evolution*, pp. 314–334, 1976.

115. M. Lynch, "The frailty of adaptive hypotheses for the origins of organismal complexity," in *Proc Natl Acad Sci USA*, vol. 104, pp. 8597–8604, 2007.

116. S. Gould and E. Vrba, "Exaptation-a missing term in the science of form," *Paleobiology*, pp. 4–15, 1982.

117. R. Dawkins, *The extended phenotype: The long reach of the gene*. Oxford University Press, 1999.

118. T. Walsh, *Timeless toys: Classic toys and the playmakers who created them*. Andrews McMeel Publishing, 2005.

119. S. Wright, "The role of mutation, inbreeding, crossbreeding, and selection in evolution," in *Proceedings of the Sixth International Congress of Genetics*, 1932.

120. J. Lehman and K. O. Stanley, "Evolving a diversity of virtual creatures through novelty search and local competition," in *GECCO '11: Proceedings of the 13th annual conference on Genetic and evolutionary computation*, (Dublin, Ireland), pp. 211–218, ACM, 12–16 July 2011.

121. S. Gould, "Planet of the bacteria," *Washington Post Horizon*, vol. 119, no. 344, p. H1, 1996.

122. W. Whitman, D. Coleman, and W. Wiebe, "Prokaryotes: the unseen majority," *Proceedings of the National Academy of Sciences*, vol. 95, no. 12, p. 6578, 1998.

123. G. Simpson, *The meaning of evolution: a study of the history of life and of its significance for man*, vol. 23. Yale University Press, 1967.

124. S. Arnott and M. Haskins, *Man Walks into a Bar: Over 6,000 of the Most Hilarious Jokes, Funniest Insults and Gut-Busting One-Liners*. Ulysses Press, 2007.

125. F.-h. Hsu, *Behind Deep Blue: Building the computer that defeated the world chess champion*. Princeton University Press, 2002.

126. J. Hooker, "Testing heuristics: We have it all wrong," *Journal of Heuristics*, vol. 1, no. 1, pp. 33–42, 1995.

127. C. Smorynski, "The incompleteness theorems," *Handbook of mathematical logic*, vol. 4, pp. 821–865, 1977.

128. J. S. Mill, *A System of Logic, Ratiocinative and Inductive*. 1846.

56195451R00093